CITY ON A HILL

VOLUME 1

THE CITY

CITY ON A HILL

Also by Ted Neill

- Science Fiction -
City on a Hill
The Selah Branch
Reaper Moon

Snog Team Six Series
Volume 1: *Jamhuri, Njambi, & Fighting Zombies*
Volume 2: *Zombies, Frat Boys, Monster Flash Mobs*
Volume 3: *HALO Jumpers, Human Traffickers, & Tiger Zombies*
Volume 4: *Glam Rockers, Glitter Bombs, Murder Birds & Emo Gods*

- Fantasy -
Elk Riders Series
Volume 1: *In the Darkness Visible*
Volume 2: *Voyage of the Elawn*
Volume 3: *The Font of Jasmeen*
Volume 4: *Journey to Karrith*
Volume 5: *The Magus*

- Illustrated Kids Books -
Mystery Force Series
Volume 1: *Mystery Force Assemble*
Volume 2: *The Case of the Stolen Horn*
Volume 3: *Blazing Blizzards*
Volume 4: *The Case of the Peryton Thief*
Volume 5: *FRAMED!*

- Non-Fiction -
Two Years of Wonder
Finding St. Lo: A Memoir of War & Family
My Name is Ted & I'm a Racist

VOLUME I – THE CITY

Tenebray Press

Published 2022. Printed in the United States of America
ISBN: 9798362371579
Cover art provided by: Agata Broncel at Bukovero Designs

CITY ON A HILL
VOLUME 1
THE CITY

BY
TED NEILL

TENEBRAY PRESS
COPYRIGHT 2022

For Chisara,

Who said, "Write it now."

According to Jewish legend there are men on earth whose righteousness before God saves all others from annihilation. They are the Lamed Vavniks. Without knowing it themselves, they are our saviors.

In Muslim tradition there are similar figures, the 40 Abdals. Both Lamed Vavniks and Abdals resemble the righteous men of Sodom in the book of Genesis. While these men, even as few as ten, stayed in Sodom, God would spare it from destruction.

VOLUME I – THE CITY

Forward

In the beginning, there was war, suffering, death. Mankind's ignorance, his clinging to superstitious fallacies nearly led to his own destruction. It is not known which side it was—all had long legacies of crimes and guilt—but one band of extremists set off the first detonation in a city that had long been the fault line for centuries of conflict. What followed was a holocaust of worldwide proportions. All life was wiped off the planet as retaliations spread from country to country, continent to continent. Cities, villages, fields, forests, streams were reduced to radioactive waste. This was called the Cataclysm. No one survived except a few hundred people just south of the first detonation.

What followed was the Transition, when our Founders denounced superstition for the rationality of law. Walls were erected around the two remaining cities: Lysander to the north and Fortinbras to the south. The old cities were razed, all signs of the past erased, and a small sliver of enlightened people started again. These, the Twin Cities, are all that is left of humanity. We have learned from our ancestors' mistakes. The nine precepts are our guide, rationality is our law, and the Head Ministry is our government. Religion is a disease.

— Twin Cities Ministry of Education, Fourth Grade Reader. Placed in all fourth grade classrooms by order of the Head Ministry.

Chapter 1

Lindsey Mehdina

"Lindsey has beetles crawling on her!" Sylvia squealed to her friends.

The four girls stood in a semicircle, cutting Lindsey off from the view of the teachers who gossiped on the far side of the playground in the shade of the school building. The building had taken on the drab colors of the playground, covered in the same dust that rose from the parched ground to settle on the goal posts, swing sets, and climbing bars—and by the end of recess—most of the children. Lindsey had put herself in this vulnerable position, choosing a distant part of the schoolyard to draw in the sand undisturbed. So isolated that she was too tempting a target for Sylvia and her gang. The nearest children were the five-year-olds—too young to help—swinging on the climbing bars. The older boys, who often liked the portraits Lindsey would draw for them, were far too engrossed in their pitchball game to notice what was unfolding.

Lindsey placed her hand over her breast pocket where she had hidden the beetles, one tumbling over the other like little gem stones. She remembered saying, "Don't hurt them," just before the seizure took her and the vision flickered before her eyes.

Once, after watching her across the breakfast table, her brother Sam told her that when she seized, her eyes tipped back in their sockets and rolled around like marbles. Her limbs shook, and sometimes snot came out of her nose. Sometimes she bit her tongue, and her teeth turned red from blood. It seemed an undignified state to her and at impossible odds with the revelations she saw with her inner eye: people, people she knew, people she had yet to know but would know. Sometimes she saw people when they were younger, often when they were older. Sometimes she saw landscapes: shady forests, heaving seas, tranquil rivers. She saw crescent moon dunes crossing deserts one grain of sand at a time. Suspended on threads of wind, she knew each grain, its golden, amber, or rose brilliance. A canyon. A cave. A thousand candles shining though glass.

Then she would come to with her cereal bowl turned over, milk on her lap, her brother resting his chin in his hand as he stared at his stopwatch.

"Forty-seven seconds," Sam said.

"It felt like eternity."

Lindsey was not sure how long this seizure and its vision had lasted. She never knew how long the visions were. She lost all sense of time. But Sylvia was staring down at her with her three friends, the sounds and shouts of other playing children continued uninterrupted, so she knew she was still at recess. No teachers' faces floated above her, so she could not have been on her back long enough to attract much attention. Lindsey tried to prop herself on her elbow, but her muscles were still not responding. She flopped back down, hitting her head. The other girls snorted and laughed.

Lindsey had braided her locks so carefully that morning, tying them with fluorescent elastics to tame the wiry curls. Now they had escaped from their bands. One stood on end waving before her face, the sun winking behind it. Her head felt as if there was a vice clamped around it. She could taste blood in her mouth and feel mucus sticking in the back of her throat. Sylvia ground one of the loose elastics into the ground.

"Your teeth will fall out, and you will be ugly the rest of your life," Lindsey said through panting breaths.

The laughing stopped.

"What did you say, you little spaz?" Sylvia said, her lip curling.

Lindsey swore inwardly. This also happened after an episode: she said thoughts out loud. Her brother always found it amusing, but it was far from funny now. Sylvia leaned in close to her, grabbed a fistful of hair, and pulled. Lindsey cried out but was unable to defend herself. She used what control she had regained in her arms to protect the beetles in her pocket. Sylvia was so close that Lindsey could feel her spit on her face. Those gray eyes, thin lips, and freckles were unmistakable. Lindsey had just seen them in her vision.

The whole of it came back then. She had been sitting on a tuft of grass, drawing in the dust with a branch. Sylvia had come over, dragging the soles of her shoes, scraping away the stars, the moons, the birds, and the butterflies Lindsey had worked so hard to render. Closer, Sylvia had spotted the beetles and cried out. Then the vision came.

It was not unusual for Lindsey to experience visions of a person standing right before her. So it did not surprise her that a piece of Sylvia's future seemed to have detached itself from the bowl of sky and fallen on her. She had seen Sylvia, her freckles faded with age, her fiery hair turned to a more subdued auburn. She was not actually ugly. Her face was lean and had lost the softness of baby fat, but she was comely in an elegant sort of way. Grown Sylvia opened her mouth to call three children—Sylvia's own children, Lindsey guessed—and where one of her front teeth should have been there was a gap.

Young Sylvia shook Lindsey back into the moment. "Did you call me ugly?"

"Ugly. So ugly. Your teeth will fall out," Lindsey muttered as if drunk. If her brother had been there, he would have been laughing. Pain spread like fire across her scalp as Sylvia pulled harder.

"Let her go."

A fifth figure had quietly walked up beside them without anyone noticing. It was the new girl, Sabrina Sabryia. She was lean and gangly, her hair always pulled back into a utilitarian pony tail, and her thick brows always furrowed into a scowl. She wore what she wore every day: a black, long-sleeved shirt and black trousers tucked into oversized boots. Her unchanging wardrobe would have made her the object of ridicule had she not arrived each day in a black ministry roll pod, long and spacious, with tinted windows, unlike the civilian roller pods (CRPs) that the other parents drove. Girls would not play with her because she looked like a boy, and boys would not play with her because she was a girl.

Lindsey, recognizing a fellow outcast, had tried talking to her once. "Your name is Annaliese," she had said.

"No, it's not. I'm Sabrina Sabryia."

"Are you sure? I saw someone call you that in a dream."

"Are you a little crazy?"

"I guess so."

Now Sabrina was studying the other girls, her eyes scanning back and forth, the muscles in her jaw working as if she was trying to crack a nut in her molars. The fabric on the elbows of her long sleeve was threadbare, as if worn from her crawling in small spaces or up trees. Her boots were scuffed and dirty, but the laces were tied with perfect, balanced precision. The other girls, in their pressed pastel dresses and plastic barrettes, could have been specimens of a different species. They crossed their arms and jutted their chins in a show of feminine solidarity.

Sabrina did not notice. Arms akimbo, standing as a teacher might, she stared at Sylvia, a little dumbfounded that the girl had not obeyed her command. Yet the pressure on Lindsey's scalp lessened, and she let out a small cry of relief.

"Why should I let her go?" Sylvia insisted. "You should mind your own business."

"What did she do to you?" Sabrina asked.

"She called me ugly."

"Did you?" Sabrina asked, turning to Lindsey.

Lindsey nodded and withered inside when she read the disapproval on Sabrina's face. But it was fleeting. Sabrina's eyes shifted to the ground. The new girl was silent a long while, turning her head, her body, even moving her feet delicately as she discovered the drawings below. Then she did something Lindsey did not expect.

Sabrina smiled.

Her smile lacked any self-consciousness, yet it looked out of place on a face that was always scowling. It floated there like an unexpected guest, lingering as Sabrina examined the work, even the images Sylvia had scuffed, as if she was trying to puzzle out what they had been before they had been destroyed. When Sabrina had completed a circuit around Lindsey, she turned to the other girls and spoke in a flat, soft, voice.

"Sylvia, if you touch her again, I'll punch you in the face."

The three other girls wore identical expressions of horror as they began to inch in the direction of the teachers. Sylvia stiffened, made to step back but then pirouetted on her foot, grabbed Lindsey's hand and crushed her fingers together. Lindsey tried to relax her grip, but it was too late. The beetles' shells cracked, and warm goo spread out of her breast pocket.

Sylvia's laugh only lasted a moment before it was cut off. Sand ground beneath the sole of Sabrina's shoe as she shifted her weight. That sound was followed by a hard, wet *smack*. The other girls were running now, screaming. Sylvia dropped to her knees beside Lindsey, holding her mouth, her two front teeth knocked askew and pink with blood. At the sight of red on her fingers, Sylvia's face grew pale. One tooth became completely detached and rolled across Sylvia's lip into her palm, where it rested like a gleaming stone. She turned to follow her friends, her shoulders beginning to shake with sobs.

"Ow," Sabrina said, rubbing her knuckles before she become aware of Lindsey staring at her, at which point she shook her hand out at her side. The boys playing pitchball on one of the more distant fields caught her attention for a moment before she turned back to the drawings at her feet.

"I can draw more if you like, Annaliese."

"I told you, my name is Sabrina," she said as she leaned over more drawings: a spiral, a moon, a fox. The fox Lindsey had drawn with dimensions and depth, but it had not turned out quite as well as she had liked. Lindsey burned with shame. Sylvia had obliterated a much better attempt of a hare. She wished Sabrina had seen that one. The teachers were coming over now, crossing the field in long strides, their arms swinging straight and fast at their sides.

"I warned her." Sabrina said with sincere wonder as she watched the teachers approach. *"I warned her.* Why would she do that?"

"It's all right," Lindsey said wiping the sticky, gleaming shells from her fingers onto her trousers. "We're going to be friends until the day we die."

"How do you know?"

A teacher arrived and yanked Sabrina's arm so hard that her feet lifted off the ground.

"I'm just often right about these things," Lindsey said as they dragged Sabrina away.

VOLUME I – THE CITY

Ten years later.

Chapter 2
Sabrina Sabryia

"Stop spinning your gun, Cadet."

Sabrina bounced the blaster upright so that it pirouetted briefly, its battery case on her knuckle, before she knocked it into her holster with a satisfied flick of her opposite hand.

"Unnecessary," Sean said.

"A question, sir."

Sean paused, his head turning a fraction of a degree towards her. The setting sun, streaming down the alleyway between buildings struck his face at such an angle that she could see his blue eyes behind his visor. The late afternoon light made his skin look tawny and the laughter lines around his eyes and mouth more prominent.

"Go ahead."

"Do you disapprove because you can't do it?" Sabrina asked, suppressing a smile.

Sean let out a gruff "Hmph" and returned to the screens projected before his eyes, his hands moving in the air in front of him as he switched between menus. "I like my face attached, that's all," he said. "Although, maybe some plasma burns could improve yours."

"I'm reporting you to my supervisor," Sabrina said, leaning against the wall and stretching her legs, the carbon fiber flex bands of her patrol suit creaking.

Sean completed his inventory of their shift assignments, lifted his visor, and started down the alleyway to the sidewalk. "Let's go, one assignment left today."

VOLUME I – THE CITY

The sun shone directly into their eyes as they turned the corner onto Carnap Avenue. Despite the glare, Sean kept his visor up and told Sabrina to do the same. "The less distance between you and the residents, the better," he said, tugging at his uniform jacket to cover up his blaster as well.

Sabrina zipped her jacket and doubled her pace to keep up with Sean's long strides. The avenue between the row houses was crowded with produce and cooking carts, each surrounded by residents stopping on their way home from work. The air smelled of rosemary and aniseed. A young girl sprayed a golden cloud of mist on a wheelbarrow of kale and turnips, turning the lime leaves and pink tubers a dark emerald and bloody red.

The moisture and the bright colors created a convincing illusion of abundance, but dust still gathered at their feet, on their sleeves, in their eyes. The desert was never far, the sand pooling in the gutters and creating a haze over their heads was a constant reminder. Occasionally Sabrina could even smell it as a breeze carrying the scent of sage and tamarisk wafted over rooftops and down an alleyway.

Sean led them into the periphery of a pitchball match, delaying long enough that when the ball rolled his way, he had a moment to juggle it up and away from the children and kick it to her. She trapped it under her foot.

"Are we dispensing with all formality?"

"Bond with the community and you'll have all the partners you ever need," Sean said. "I do have the highest rate of solved cases in the station, and it's not because of my interrogation techniques."

Sabrina tipped the ball onto the top of her foot, before toeing it to her knees, her thighs, then her head where she balanced it for a few moments. The children cheered when she kicked it back to them.

"Look," Sean said, nodding across the street to where the children's mothers were also clapping for her. Sabrina felt her cheeks flush. "Don't be embarrassed. They are proud of you. How many of them do you think wanted to play sports when they were younger, or even wanted to join the Security Ministry?"

Sabrina fell back into a steady pace beside him. "I can't be responsible for all their hopes and dreams."

"But you are," Sean said, breaking stride for a moment to look her in the face. She felt a stirring within her, a tremor from her mouth down to the base of her spine when he turned his sharp, clear eyes to her. "You are. And you're ready, too. Tell me about our friend Mr. Elias Orehem."

"Repair shop owner, 23 years of age," she said matching his stride again. "No prior arrests or citations. A few disciplinary actions while in school, nothing unusual for a non-academically inclined teenage boy. Apprenticed briefly as a machinist before inheriting his uncle's shop here. Has not attended any tertiary education."

"And your visor is up, you are reciting this from memory," Sean said glancing sidelong at her.

"I studied our daily mission briefing last night," she said.

"And I thought you spent all your time just practicing twirling your gun."

"That is only when you are talking, sir." Sean laughed, and Sabrina felt the tremor return with a pleasant rush.

"Why are we paying him a visit?" he asked.

"The pharmacy on Grayling Street is suspected of distilling illegal spirits. There have been reports of late night activity during quiet hours, and rates of violent incidents have increased in the neighborhood. The reports center around the shop," she said.

"Why is this important?"

"Rates of violent crime sometimes portend cult activity, although there have never been any reports of it in this neighborhood."

"Never say never," Sean said, studying the addresses of the houses.

Sabrina slowed enough that Sean came to a stop a few feet ahead and turned back to look at her, the flow of pedestrians parting around them. "Is there a point I am missing?"

The corner of Sean's mouth twisted downward, and he rubbed the late day shadow of whiskers on his face. "To be honest, I don't know."

Foot traffic continued to pass on either side of them: men with their vests folded over their arms, their underarms dark with perspiration; women with their hair pinned up to expose necks glistening with sheens of sweat; and children, their book satchels bouncing on their hips. Sabrina wanted to slip her own uniform jacket off, but it would expose her weapon and her patrol suit. Wrapped in carbon mesh armor, flex bands, and servo plates, Sean was right: they would look removed from the daily scene playing out around them.

"I'm not sure what you mean," Sabrina said, raising her hand to her face to block the sun.

Sean stepped closer to her and spoke in a lower register, "What do you *think* of Elias Orehem?"

"I tried not to form any premature conclusions."

"Good. That's what you are trained to do. Now forget your training."

"Forget my training?"

"Yep. Your gut tells you something. What?"

She raked through the information in her mind again but could come up with nothing. "Elias Orehem is relatively unremarkable."

"You are exactly right," Sean said. "He is completely unremarkable, and that is remarkable, isn't it?"

"I'm not sure I get you."

"There may be nothing to *get*. He could just be a humble guy of limited ambition, in a humble profession, in a humble shop."

"So I was concluding," Sabrina said.

"But most young men I have known have some degree of ambition. Nothing feeds the ego like youth and naïveté. How many would be content to work in a little shop on this street the rest of their lives?"

"Maybe he aspires to start more shops."

"Good observation. Keep it in mind when you interrogate him." Sean nodded toward a set of stairs leading to the basement of a row house next to them. "After you."

"This is the place?" Sabrina asked, looking up at the row house. It had been refurbished since the Transition with new light fixtures and a fresh coat of standard ministry-approved paint. The basement door, however, looked as if it belonged to a different building. Paint peeled off its face in long curled leaves, revealing rusted metal beneath.

"Cadet," Sean smiled. "You've done the leg work. You interrogate him. I'm going to look for a new gyroscope for my CRP."

Sabrina opened her mouth to speak but could not find the words. After a few aborted attempts she stopped completely, aware that she likely resembled a fish gasping for air.

"Yes, Sir," she finally said.

The bottom of the door screeched on the floor as she freed it from the jamb. The air on the other side smelled of copper, oil, and dirt. The space was dark; the window at ground level was clouded with sand and dust. If Elias Orehem had ambitions for his shop, they were not apparent in the haphazard way items were thrown together on the sagging, overcrowded shelves. Vacuum tubes, fuel blenders, gyroscopes, hovers, suspensor clamps—many covered in cobwebs—all vied for shelf space. Sean gravitated towards the shelves holding tired-looking gyroscopes, nodding at Sabrina to continue.

She navigated around more overcrowded tables and tilting shelves and stopped at a worn counter in the back of the shop. A stick of incense was burning in a pot of dirt. In the stale air, the smoke hovered, undisturbed, in a wispy layer at the level of her head. Sabrina heard a noise, a tinkling of metal on metal, behind the beaded curtain that led to the back of the shop. She called out. "Hello, Mr. Orehem?"

Footsteps shuffled in back before a young man with chalky skin and long, lean features parted the beads with one hand. Dark circles ringed the skin below his eyes. His hair was slicked back and ran down to his collar.

"Yes?" He offered a tentative smile.

He was still only halfway through the curtain. He wore a light scarf and a floor-length jacket to ward off the damp cold of the basement. An oil rag hung from his pants pocket, and a belt of wrenches was strapped beneath it.

"I am Cadet Sabryia. That is Officer Maher over there in your gyroscope aisle," she said pointing over her shoulder with her thumb.

"I might have some questions about one of these when you are finished," Sean said with a good-natured grin.

"Certainly," Orehem laughed, a jagged sound that came from the back of his throat.

"You are Mr. Orehem, the owner of this shop?" Sabrina said, trying to return some formality to the conversation.

"Yes, I am," he said, shifting his eyes back and forth between her and Sean.

"We're here to ask about some reports of neighborhood disturbances, mainly centered around the pharmacy a few doors down."

"Disturbances," he said smiling, his body rocking back and forth slightly as he wiped his hands on his oil rag. "Like what?"

"Loud, uncivilized behavior. Customers coming late at night. Even fights."

"None of that. I've seen nothing. It's a quiet neighborhood." He bent down to adjust the incense stick.

Sabrina felt something tighten within her. He was lying. "Mr. Orehem, how long have you owned this shop?"

"Why?" he said, moving his hand from the incense stick to roll the beads of the curtain between his fingers.

"Well, it just seems like an established business, but you seem young, close to my age actually. I'm just wondering, did you run it while you were in school?"

"My uncle … he recently died, and I inherited it," he said.

"I was raised by my uncle. He is like a father to me." She smiled. "Do you normally work late or leave early?"

"I, uh, I work late, yes. I'm often here late."

"Regularly, and you have never heard any of the noises the neighbors have complained about that I mentioned earlier?"

The tendons in his neck twitched. He was making a fist around the beads in his hands.

"Why is it of interest to you?" he asked.

"Well as you know, Mr. Orehem, when neighbors complain about such activities around a pharmacy, the first thing authorities suspect is an illegal distillery. Do you know the owner of the pharmacy in question?"

"I've seen him around, I keep to myself. I don't interact with him."

"You don't. No shopkeeper guild of any sort?"

"I'm not a member. I'm here usually."

Sabrina noted where the touch of her hand had smeared away dust from the counter. Sean knocked over something on a shelf. Orehem snapped his head in Sean's direction. His knuckles were white around the beads. Sabrina felt her own heart beating harder in her chest.

Remain calm. Don't upset the subject.

"You are here a lot," she said.

"Yes."

"Most of your work is in the back of the shop?"

"You need authorization to search my shop," he said, raising his voice. Sean's footsteps moved closer.

"We're not here to search your premises, Mr. Orehem. Just ask questions. You've been quite helpful," she said.

Sean moved up alongside her, holding a gyroscope in either hand. "You don't have a third one in back do you?"

Sean's attempt to diffuse the tension came too late. Orehem slipped from between the string of beads and jumped the counter. A number of strands came loose, raining beads down on the floor. Sabrina saw a flash in Orehem's hand, and she knew exactly what had cut the curtain.

"Sean, knife!"

Sean raised his arm to restrain Orehem. Orehem swung the knife directly into Sean's armpit. The gyroscopes dropped to the floor as Sean grabbed Orehem by his jacket and flung him away from his body. Orehem raised the bloody knife again, but Sean knocked Orehem's arm away and charged in close, both of them crashing into the shelves. The shelves collapsed, and an avalanche of unsold merchandise tumbled down around them. Rubber hoses, motor housing, and intake ducts flew as both men kicked to extricate themselves. Sabrina raced over the wreckage, tripping and falling, her head slamming against a drawer full of wrenches. Woozy, she squeezed herself between fallen shelves and tried to tackle Orehem. The shopkeeper recovered before she could catch him and leapt out of her reach, bolting for the stairs. The rusty door clanged shut as his feet disappeared up the steps.

"*Crite!*" Sean swore, holding his side. He swore again when he saw the blood on his hand. "Suit can withstand a plasma blast, but he gets me with a knife."

"The suits should hold up to a knife."

"There are weak spots," Sean said, rolling out of the debris and touching his hand to his armpit again. "*Crite.* He knew just where it was, too."

The suit had registered the breach to its structural integrity. A computerized voice in Sabrina's ear informed her that filament sensors in Sean's suit had detected the chemical signature of blood. A cascade of protocols was activating. Derm links relayed Sean's vitals to network operators at the station. Officers within a predetermined radius were receiving their location and Sean's vital signs as they spoke. The noise was too much for her, and Sabrina yanked out her ear piece. She ripped open a pocket on her thigh, removed a sterile adhesive patch and slapped it on Sean's wound so abruptly that he cried out.

"Put your headset back on," Sean said between gasps.

She did. Squawking voices and alarms inundated her again. Everything was moving too quickly. She flipped down her visor. Sean and her vitals ran across the bottom of her field of vision. Her heart rate was skyrocketing. So was Sean's, but at least it was steady. He pulled his visor down and began speaking into his filament microphone.

Sabrina changed the readouts before her and became absorbed in the map flashing before her eyes. It displayed their position: two white dots in a skeleton frame of roads and buildings. The perspective zoomed out so she could see two blue dots: a medic unit moving in their direction; two green dots, the nearest two officers. She swore when she saw their names in bold script, tracing their progress through the streets: Pitt and Boyle.

Sean relayed the description of his attacker to the operator at the station. More green units, more names she knew, began to converge on their location, like iron filings drawn to a magnet. He finished, muted his microphone, and signaled for Sabrina to do the same. He began speaking in a quick but deliberate tone. "This is the first attack on an officer since your cohort started at the academy."

"An attack on an officer is a class two offense. It is—"

"An attack on the Ministry itself, yeah I know. Do you know what that translates into?

"A minimum sentence of six months," she said. "It means two years of behavioral supervision."

"It means he's dead."

"What?"

"*Think,* Cadet. He won't make it back to the station. The old guard is going to want to set an example for the new guard."

"They will kill him?"

"He will resist. It will be justified. Every report will corroborate, and every visor camera will be conveniently switched off or blocked. With all the arrests lately in the Blocks, all the fights, no one will question it."

"That's murder."

"That is justice, as far as our colleagues are concerned. Welcome to the officer corps."

Sabrina swallowed hard. Her hands were shaking. She crouched on the floor and began to pull on her bootlaces, twisting their ends around her fingers as if the tightness could still the shaking. The stairway remained empty on the far side of the door.

"But that's not me, and I know it's not you," Sean added.

"You're still injured. What can we do?"

"Not we, but you. You've got to save him. Make it right."

"He just tried to kill you!"

"Is justice settling the score? I've taught you better."

A series of choices played out in her mind. Her partner was injured, and it was her fault. The man who had done it had escaped and was sure to be killed. But death-by-officer was not true justice.

"A cadet is not allowed to pursue an armed suspect alone," she said.

"For *crite* sake, Sabrina, I'll cover for you. Why is a repair shop owner attacking a bucket-head officer playing with his gyroscopes? He's hiding something, and we'll never find out if we—*you*—don't catch him."

"You're right," she said. She checked the map on her visor. The medics were five blocks away, blue dots rolling through a fine-lined maze. A ring of green was closing quickly. The medics would be there in three minutes. She checked Sean's vitals again. The last thing she needed, after getting her partner injured, was a reputation for abandoning him in critical condition. But he was not in danger. The patch had stopped the bleeding. His vitals were stable.

"Go," he said waving at the door.

"Sean—Sir, I can't leave you."

"Don't make me point my gun at you."

She made her decision, or recognized it had been made for her. Another avalanche of junk tumbled down as she clambered over the fallen shelves to the door and tried the handle. It was locked from the outside. The patrol suit, following the movement of her eyes through her visor, was already superimposing information about the metal of the door. The surface was fatigued, but the interior was still strong. It would take too many blasts of plasma to melt through. Red lines traced the outline of the bolts that formed the door's locking mechanism. Most of them were deep in the interior. Such a heavy door and reinforced lock belonged on a vault, not a dusty repair shop. Sean was right: they had stumbled into something. The owners had something to hide.

She checked the window. Too small. Scans also revealed it to be reinforced.

Think, Sabrina.

The ceiling consisted of wood rafters. Using the visor again, she peeled away layers. The floor above the rafters was wood with nothing but a laminate surface on top. A further scan on infrared revealed the house to be empty of any inhabitants.

She drew her blaster, flicked the setting with her thumb and fired. A red bolt struck the ceiling with a loud thud, followed by the crackle of wood disintegrating in intense heat. The basement suddenly smelled like a campfire. A column of ashes, dust, and charred wood fell on her. Shooting at an angle would have been better, she scolded herself. The suit could help her make an augmented jump, but she opted instead for her grapple. A second scan revealed a pipe was embedded in the ceiling. She raised her arm, locked her elbow, and fired the grappling device from her wrist.

VOLUME I – THE CITY

Five metal talons folded like a tight bud punched through the ceiling before blooming and seizing the pipe. The line extending from her wrist relayed sensory information into the fingers of her glove. She could "feel" the smooth cold metal surface of the pipe and the grinding of plaster dust as she closed the talon around it. Before she tugged on the line to activate the winches built into the shoulder of the suit, she glanced at Sean. He jerked his thumb upwards.

"Go."

Chapter 3

Pursuit

She pulled the line and zipped onto the next floor. She was in the foyer. Shoes waited in a neat row for their owners, their types and colors representing each member of the family. A coat rack held a number of deflated rain jackets. Afternoon light spilled into the adjacent room through gossamer curtains while empty couches waited for their occupants. A child's doll rested face down on a coffee table next to reading tablets and a toy roll pod.

After releasing their grip, the grappling talons relaxed, and the line whipped back into the casing on her forearm. Sabrina turned the bolt in the door, stepped out onto the front steps, and descended into the street. She asked two children where the man who had just come up the stairs had gone. They pointed right.

It was hopeless. Among the playing children, evening commuters, market sellers, Orehem was nowhere to be seen.

Sabrina had already lost precious time. Oreham had a sizable lead. Sean had had no chance to slap a tracking device on him. She looked with growing despair at the long street, crowded with people and broken by dozens of cross streets and alleyways. The ring of green beacons was growing tighter by the moment. Her skin felt hot beneath her suit.

He could be anywhere, she thought. Running blindly down the road would be of little use, especially if she passed some point where he had turned off. A child kicked a ball towards the sticks that were set up as a goal in the ongoing game of pitchball. Other children chased after it in long strides.

Think, Sabrina. Think. She switched her visor to infrared, turning the people on the street into ghostly blobs of orange surrounded by halos of red. The cobblestone street was a deep purple, almost black. She increased the sensitivity, and the heat the pavement had absorbed from the sun's rays appeared in a soft blue. Another increase of sensitivity, and the imprints from footsteps swelled into view—heat left by the friction of soles on the stones. The children stamped chaotic orange prints around their game. Casual walkers left cooling yellow prints in evenly spaced rows. She studied the mosaic at her feet until she found a faint trail of fading prints, a cooler blue subsiding into indigo, spaced far apart, like those of a runner.

She launched herself, dodging and weaving around pedestrians, her velocity boots amplifying her leg's exertions so that her body hurled over more ground between strides. The color of the footsteps was already changing to a greener, warmer hue. On her earpiece, the operator's voice recited ministry guidelines forbidding a cadet to pursue a violent suspect without supervision, but Scan cut in with exaggerated cries of pain.

Sabrina's pulse had settled into a steady drumming, but she was not tired. She had trained too much for that. The footsteps turned to the left, and she followed them through an alleyway into the next street. The previous street was reserved for pedestrians, but this one was open to traffic. Cool indigo spheres—civilian roll pods—whirred past, their occupants warm orange blobs and their fuel cells a hot white beneath their seats. The trail of steps cut through the lanes of traffic and the opposite curb. Sabrina followed, dodging vehicles, ignoring horns. Tires screeched, and two roll pods collided. She kept running, following the trail of steps into an alleyway. The footprints were a forest green. In places, they were very close together, as if Orehem had slowed to look over his shoulder. She hurdled reclamation bins and broken furniture. The steps turned the corner, ran along the storefronts of the next street before crossing traffic at an angle. She followed, dodging through another gauntlet of commuters headed home. After the next turn, she knew where she was headed. The pavement here was cracked, the streets narrower, and the buildings drab. She was entering the oldest section of the city, the Blocks.

The apartments were too small, the streets and alleys too narrow, the people insubordinate. She knew the streets and alleys well from many trips to investigate disturbances. The sounds of crying children and a fighting couple drifted down to her from the building above while she weaved about un-reclaimed trash. Around another corner, she tripped and crashed onto the ground, her feet caught by a man passed out, his legs stretched out across the gutter. The collision did not even wake him. He was passed out from illegal spirits. His clothes were ragged, and a pungent scent of urine hung over him. She contemplated slapping restraints on him that very moment so she could come back to pick him up, but her thoughts froze when she saw the words scribbled on the wall behind him.

Theopin will set us free.

Even in the midst of pursuit, her body hot and streaked with perspiration, the words sent a chill though her. Illegal. Religious. Toxic. She made a note to return and investigate with Sean.

Another corner and another street. The Blocks, for all their notoriety, were not all too different in their daily rhythms from the newer neighborhoods. On Diagoras Street, one of the wider boulevards, she passed residents on their way home. Children played tag and kicked balls. Street venders sold vegetables and flat breads from carts. Residents glanced up, startled, as she ran past.

The footsteps were a bright green now. She was very close. Her quarry had even stopped running. The spacing of this steps told Sabrina that he had slowed to a fast walk. *Why had he come here?* She asked herself. Was it his home? Did he have friends? If that was the case, she could be in danger. As she turned into the next alleyway, she drew her blaster and depressed the setting to stun. The steps were normally spaced now, passing close to one side of the alley, avoiding the gutter of waste water than ran down the center. She took deep breaths to help her body recover. The steps disappeared around a corner. Instead of following outright, her instincts kept her back. She peered around the building.

He was there, stopped, leaning over, his hands on his knees, gulping air. Before turning the corner, Sabrina scanned the space above. Five stories of metal balconies loomed overhead, each crowded with fire escape ladders, potted plants, and outdoor furniture. Laundry hung on sagging lines between them. She detected no sinister allies of the man waiting to get the jump on her. She lifted the blaster and stepped out.

"Put your hands over your head, Orehem!" she shouted. Surprise and terror mixed on his face. He had nowhere to go. The end of the alleyway was blocked by a wire mesh fence. Sabrina kept the blaster trained on him, waiting for him to cooperate, but his luck had not run out just yet: a gray haired woman, wearing a floral dress and work apron, stepped through a doorway into the space between them. She was followed by a girl who could have been her grandchild. Both carried baskets of laundry on their heads and were civilians that could not be stunned without great risk. Orehem sensed his opportunity and raced down the alley. Sabrina cursed, pushing past the startled bystanders. It was too late to fire. The shopkeeper had already scaled the fence at the end of the alleyway and disappeared into the space beyond.

Sabrina holstered her weapon and tore off her outer jacket. It was more ornamental than not and what mattered now was exposing her entire patrol suit. She charged the fence and carried out a series of movements with her hands. Sensors in her gloves recorded the flexing of her fingers, and thousands of microscopic filaments in her suit tensed and spread, tickling her skin as the patrol suit prepared to climb. She pivoted and continued running up the face of the wall, the suit adhering and releasing in time with her motions. The bricks rained flakes down upon her, but the suit held until she neared the ground on the other side of the fence. More flexing of her fingers and the adhesive filaments relaxed. She fell, rolled to disperse her momentum, then resumed pursuit.

The desert yawned open around them, red light from the setting sun streaking across the hardpan. The map superimposed on her field of vision showed her own white dot moving outside the circuitry of the city streets. A solitary star in the blackness of space. Orehem was running eastward, into the blazing inferno of the setting sun, the flaps of his jacket snapping in his wake like dark wings. Sabrina followed. Orehem saw her over his shoulder and altered his course toward a hulking structure that Sabrina could not make out in the glare. She increased the filter on the visor and recognized the silhouette to be the barrier surrounding a new ramp of highway still under construction.

She threw herself over the temporary walls and started up the empty road that led directly into the fiery sky. Orehem had not broken stride and continued over a rise in the ramp, disappearing down the other side. The sound of traffic was already filling her ears. Over the crest, the road sloped downward. Orehem had stopped where it ended, its paved surface giving way to exposed rebar that waited to be covered in cement. Six lanes of evening traffic shot across the Coast Road below. Beyond, the sea waited, dark as ink.

Sabrina switched her blaster to her left hand. It was not her firing hand. Stunning him was out of the question while he stood so close to the edge. Instead, she readied her grapple and moved in slow, measured steps.

"Mr. Orehem, please. I have no intention to hurt you," she said between deep breaths of air. "Please, step away from the edge. I am sure this is a misunderstanding."

She wanted to sound calm, but she could hear the tension in her words. Other voices were clamoring, calling on her ear piece. She ripped it out so that the roar of traffic filled her head from both sides, like the sudden onrush of an ocean wave.

"Mr. Orehem, please, we just came to ask you questions about distilleries."

A yellow CRP cut off a blue one on the motorway. The ensuing honk rose and faded, the frequency warbling with the speed. Sabrina moved deliberately, placing her weapon back in her holster in exaggerated movements. "See, I don't mean to shoot you, Mr. Orehem."

He copied her same motions, turning around slowly, but remaining close to the edge. His heels cantilevered just over the lip of road. He kept his hands away from his body, his palms upwards to the red sky. His chest was rising and falling from exertion. Sweat poured down his face and soaked his shirt. His expression had changed since she had caught him unawares in the alleyway. Now he seemed calm, serene even. Sabrina thought he might just surrender, until she saw the glint of gold on his chest. In his flight, his shirt had come open and resting there on his drenched skin, in a nest of dark hair was a tiny gold sword. It glinted in the sunlight, and the beam struck Sabrina in the eye like a golden nail. Her body went rigid and she felt cold, just as she had when she had seen those words written in the alleyway.

She swallowed, but could not bring herself to speak. She regretted holstering her blaster.

Mr. Orehem looked steadily into her eyes, as if he knew exactly what she saw and what she was thinking. Before he stepped backwards, he smiled widely and spoke, "Into your weapons, I send my ghost."

He fell backwards, arms outstretched, face upturned to the sky. Sabrina broke out of her shock to shoot the grappling hook at his feet as they tipped over the edge. Her aim was accurate, but just before the talons could reach his leg, they ricocheted off a finger of exposed rebar and arced upwards in an oblique path. When the talons brushed his jacket collar, Sabrina clenched her fist and the metal prongs clamped down, the sensation of fabric running under her fingers. With a jerking motion, she yanked the slack out of the line and braced herself.

VOLUME I – THE CITY

The weight was more than she could have ever anticipated. Only her patrol suit kept her arm from being dislocated. Her body slammed down onto the concrete, and her suit made a zipping noise as she was dragged across the road's surface. Panic welled up inside her as she uselessly kicked out her legs. She had just anchored herself to a man trying to kill himself, and physics was on his side. Her body folded around the lip of the unfinished road, her feet dangling over the passing traffic. Servos in the suit vibrated and whined in her armpits and hips as they tried to augment her arms' strength. Her chest felt as if it would break in two as the line holding Orehem swung from one arm, and she clung to rebar with the other. Her hand began to slip until the adhesive grip reactivated. She knew the suit could maintain her grip until reinforcements arrived, but she was not sure the talons would hold Orehem. His jacket was tented over his head while he swayed, kicking, each movement sending a spasm of pain up through Sabrina. If she had a third arm, she would have stunned him, but instead she had to watch helplessly as he twisted, turned and slipped out of his jacket.

She closed her eyes, but she still heard everything. The abrupt disappearance of his weight was followed by a bang like a heavy sack of sand hitting concrete and popping open. Tires screeched. Metal crashed. A suspensor lorry blew its horn. A trailer rolled end-over-end. Glass windscreens popped and shattered. Something huge and metal tumbled. After the commotion came the voices. Voices yelling in the earpiece on her collar. Voices from the roadway below. A woman screamed.

Sabrina opened her eyes and turned her face from the chaos below to the horizon where the setting sun was igniting the sea the color of blood.

Chapter 4

L'ved

Chaos.

Screaming. In Sabrina's ear. Screaming faces all around her. A woman wailing behind a shattered windscreen. A small boy seated against a tire, knees hugged against his chest. Other civilians pressing in against her.

"My son is hurt."

"What the *crite* was that guy doing?"

"Did he fall or jump?"

"Has some one called the medics?"

"Get back, I need a perimeter," Sabrina said.

"That guy is not breathing."

"Are you all right?"

"Call security."

"She is security."

"What is wrong with her?"

". . .perimeter, I need a perimeter. . ." she said.

"She's a kid."

"Just a cadet."

"Get a real officer."

"Please, my son. He is hurt." One man who was more insistent than the others had pushed through the crush of people to grab her hand—still sore from gripping the rebar. His own face covered in blood, a glittering snow of broken glass dusting his hair. Blood stained his shirt collar. She braced herself for the sight of his child. "Please call help," he said, his eyes pleading.

She pressed the earpiece to her ear, and a flood of voices filled her head, a dozen cross conversations, officers calling in positions, operators reciting coordinates and protocols. She attempted to speak over them, identifying herself as the cadet, officer, at the scene. She stumbled over the words. Before she could continue all the voices went silent as a hand ripped the visor and earpiece from her head and threw them to the pavement. Officer Pitt's face was in her own.

"What the *crite* did you think you were doing?"

Pitt's eyes were wide with rage. His spit misted on her own mouth, causing her to sneer involuntarily. An artery was throbbing in his flushed neck, and his nostrils flared with each breath. The cartilage in his nose and ears was uneven and flattened from years of grappling training and his own off-duty brawls. Sabrina had never grappled with him in class, but she suspected the first time could be coming any moment.

"I was pursuing the suspect," Sabrina said, straightening her back.

"Cadets are not authorized to pursue an armed suspect alone."

"I must have missed that lecture, sir."

The mesh of his gloves creaked as he flexed his fist. "Want to miss them all?"

"Please," a loud voice cut in. For a moment Sabrina broke eye contact to look to the civilians, each one staring with incredulity at the sight of two security personnel arguing. Again, it was the man with the bloody collar and hurt son who begged them to do their jobs.

"Please, someone, can you help my—"

He could not finish his sentence before Abner, Pitt's cadet, moved to block him with his arm, pushing him towards the crowd, an indifferent expression on his face. "Step back, we need perimeter. This is a crime scene."

Sabrina had experienced the same indifference from Abner herself. Even though she had helped him train and pass the hand-to-hand combat exam—he had sought her help after failing it the first time—since being assigned to Pitt, he acted as if he had never known her.

"The crime is that he is yelling at her when we need help!" the man shouted.

The words were barely out of his mouth before he was shoved backwards, his head snapping forward with such force that his chin bounced off his chest before he landed on the roadway several feet away. Sabrina knew that the officer who had shoved him had done so with the augmented strength of the patrol suit—unnecessary and cruel—but it effectively silenced the crowd. Sabrina wanted to strip her own suit off, hand in her trainee badge, and stand with the civilians, she was so disgusted.

It was Pitt's partner, Boyle, who stood over the man now, glowering at the stunned on-lookers. He ran his thumb and forefinger down either side of his mouth, smoothing his beard. Pitt's shoulders shook, and he snorted and laughed.

Sabrina had had enough. She swiped up her visor. As she stood up, a third officer arrived, recognized her as a cadet and asked her to sit off to the side on a guardrail.

"No problem. I didn't come here to beat up civilians anyway," she said and shouldered her way past Pitt.

VOLUME I – THE CITY

The desert was at her back, like a crouched jackal, whose breath of tamarisk and hyssop wafted over her shoulder on a harsh breeze. The heat of the day still radiated from the rocks at her feet, even though the air had turned cold. The sun had set over the eastern horizon, the light globes clicked on overhead, lighting up the roadway. She re-collected her pony tail, and tied and untied her boots. The fidgeting kept her from simply dropping her head into her hands—a show of emotion she knew she could not indulge in now. Too many eyes watching. Too many men waiting to see the female cadet break. Instead she crossed, re-crossed, and yanked her laces. When her visor vibrated beside her, she picked it up.

"You all right?" Sean asked.

"I should ask you that."

"I'm stable. The medics patched me up. Then got diverted to the highway."

"Sean, I'm sorry he jumped. I tried grappling him—"

"We'll talk later. Look at this."

An inset appeared in her vision, and she enlarged it with a flick of her fingers. It was the feed from Sean's visor. He was brushing aside a beaded curtain.

"You're still at the scene."

"Yep. And we've really kicked the hornet's nest. Here," he said bending down. She fought off the disorientation that came as Sean's perspective turned and dipped. He was kneeling down beside a wood wall panel that looked as if it had already been pried open. He slid it aside then flicked on his palm light to reveal pegs full of glittering gold necklaces with sun, moon, and sword pendants. "We were certainly on to something."

"I'll say. He was wearing one of those before he jumped. The T-heads come?"

"Didn't even bother. One of the ravens alighted on this very street. Already extracted all the video files from my headset. Scared the neighbors witless."

"Is it still there?"

"If it were, I wouldn't be in this house. I have no doubt that he's on his way to see you with a host of T-heads.'

"I'll bet," Sabrina said with a sinking feeling in the pit of her stomach. "Sean, he cursed me."

The line was quiet a moment before Sean took a deep breath, "Don't let that bother you, it's just superstition. We got to stomp this *crot* out."

"Yeah."

"You did good, Cadet. I'm sorry, I had no idea. I didn't think he'd do something like that."

"I know, I didn't either."

"Don't worry. We'll get you a new blaster, just to start a clean slate."

"Thanks."

"And Sabrina,"

"Yeah."

"Stay away from that machine, all right? Those things they're—well, evil." He laughed sheepishly.

"A little superstitious yourself, sir."

"Can't find a better word. But I just don't like them. Stay away."

"Yes, sir."

The link went dead. Sabrina pulled up a map of her surroundings. Blue and green dots representing security and medical personnel floated before her eyes like cells beneath a microscope. She clicked upwards, reducing the scene so that what was a jumble became a narrow clump of lights on a thread of roadway. The desert to the west. The sea to the east. At 500 feet a black dot, only visible by its gold outline, swung into her perspective, circling, like a raven over a corpse.

An L'ved.

She ripped off the visor and looked up with her naked eyes. The blue glow of the machine's methaline engines was visible and growing. Immediately in front of her, a black all-terrain van with mirrored windows, knobby tires, and a raised chassis screeched to a stop. A half dozen men, in suits like her own, except gray, wearing helmets with T-shaped visors leapt out, slamming doors behind them so hard that the vehicle shook.

The security officers and medics froze. A quick flick with her fingers returned the overhead view, and Sabrina could watch as each blue and green dot became still and waited for a gray one to near before moving again. Pitt presented himself to the T-head—so called for the T-shaped visors—and was the model of civility and obedience. It made Sabrina want to spit. At the Head Ministry, she had grown up around the T-heads, or T-men, as her uncle called his agents. She had no better knowledge of who they were than her fellow officers and while she also disliked them, she was not intimidated.

But she was worried one might recognize her and reveal the secret of who she really was.

The T-heads erected monomer sheeting around the perimeter of the accident site in order to conceal it. Sabrina turned her face upwards again. Against the stars, with its wings outstretched, the L'ved did indeed resemble a carrion bird. She followed its spiraling trajectory by the pale blue light of its thrusters, which whined like a chorus of screaming children. The sound reached the bystanders and medical personnel, and they retreated to a more comfortable distance behind the ruined vehicles. Nobody liked the L'veds. Sabrina noticed even Abner turning and fleeing, the backwash of the engines swirling the dust and debris at his feet.

The machine descended further until it hovered right over the accident scene. The concealment sheeting snapped loudly. Sabrina's hair whipped into her eyes. Dried bushes and weeds along the shoulder of the road twisted and crackled. A bank of lights on the machine's chest powered on and stabbed into the darkness. The monomer sheeting was transformed into a gold wall with ghostly misshapen shadows thrown against it. The thrusters closed with a sound akin to a breath being cut off, leaving just the soft decrescendo of slowing turbines. The ground vibrated and glass crunched as the L'ved touched down and began to move.

It towered above the sheeting, walking like a giant among men, its wings folded back and its arms resting at its sides, its face an impervious convex mask of smoked glass concealing sensor arrays, electronic eyes, and recording devices. The shadows continued to move to and fro across the sheeting. The officers were beholden to the T-men, the T-men to the L'ved. The machine stalked through the wreckage of the scene, its face turned away from Sabrina, but she knew that meant little. It was watching her. It was watching everybody. She remembered Sean's words, his orders, to stay away. But she found she could not restrain herself. L'ved or no L'ved, it was her accident scene, her mess, her investigation. She left the guardrail, pulled aside the sheeting, and stepped through.

Once inside, her courage evaporated. A twisting feeling returned to her stomach, and she struggled not to betray the light, insubstantial sensation of weakness coursing through her limbs. Investigators spread crystalline powder onto the pools of blood on the road surface. Others ran scanners over the ground. She saw no other cadets within the sheeting. Boyle stood on the periphery beside a terrified lorry driver. The lorry itself was tipped on its side, headlights off, engine silent, suspensor magnets dark and collapsed. Sabrina thought of a dead animal. Officers moved around it inspecting the jumbled cargo of aquifer couplers, storage cylinders, and charcoal-iodine filters. With all the activity, one could almost forget the lonely body left in the center of the enclosure, except for the sentient machine looming over it. The L'ved appeared to have a special interest in the body of the occultist. It loomed over Orehem like an obsidian tree that had taken root at the scene of death.

No one noticed her, and she attempted to act as if she belonged. She tried to remember her crime scene training. Out of instinct, she inspected the ground along the path of the lorry. The tires had scorched the road surface and left shreds of rubber in their wake. Patches of concrete were dark with blood. Next to one stain something flashed in the passing light of a medic. Sabrina activated her own palm light, and the weight of cold fear returned.

The chain was broken, but the miniature sword lay on the ground just beside it. She recorded the image with her visor, then picked it up. Even with gloves on, she recoiled as if clutching a roach.

"Cadet Sabryia."

Pitt was standing over her. His hair, which had begun to thin, was closely cropped and she could see a sheen of sweat glistening on his scalp. He was missing the swagger from earlier, but she could sense the edge in his voice at finding her within the concealment sheeting. She was saved by a T-man who walked up alongside them.

"I found a piece of evidence," she said, holding out the necklace for the T-man to examine. The corner of Pitt's mouth twitched. "He was wearing this before he jumped," she added.

"You are the cadet who followed him," the T-man asked. The glass was down on his visor so she could not see his face, but she was sure he had likely seen her a dozen times before at the Head Ministry. She swallowed and hoped he would treat her with the same indifference his colleagues exhibited toward her.

"I am."

"Come with me, both of you."

He led them towards the L'ved, which still stood over Orehem's body. A curved portion of exoskeleton with a white number 6 indicated the machine's identity. The L'ved's microphones would have already picked up the sound of her voice. Her heart rate, skin temperature, even perspiration rate would be routed through liquid sodium circuitry and analyzed along stored algorithms in order to anticipate her behavior. She jumped when green light momentarily blinded her—a laser from the L'ved's mid-section. She remembered that this was how the L'veds saw faces. As if this data weighed more than the rest it had collected, the L'ved shifted slightly, turning its body towards her and inclining its head. Sabrina's skin prickled. The fuel cells, coolant circulators, and joint motors that were the internal organs of the machine hummed as it moved closer.

"Show it what you found," The T-man said.

Sabrina had never been so close to one of the machines before. Even at the Head Ministry they never were more than black specks circling in the air far above, the whine of their engines barely audible between the occasional breaking of ocean waves. She held out the necklace and the sword. The L'ved's hydraulics hissed as it moved closer. Was *it* interested or was some T-man in a dark room miles away, tapping a joy stick and leaning closer to his monitor, interested?

The machine shifted away again, turning its attention back to the body. The T-man took the necklace from Sabrina and pocketed it. "Can you identify the body, please," he asked.

Sabrina nodded and turned to Orehem. His arms and legs were broken, bent at odd angles. Abrasions had torn muscle into a bloody pulp. Splintered bones broke through his skin. The smell of fear and sweat mixed with the raw meat odor of a butcher shop. Regret was building within Sabrina until she saw his face. It was serene, beatific even, mocking her. Something shifted inside her, as deep as her bowels. She wanted to vomit, kick his face in until it was as bloody and broken as his limbs. Her eyes flashed with green as the L'ved studied her expression. She reminded herself that she was being observed and put forth her most professional demeanor.

"It's him," she said. The T-man and the L'ved seemed to confer, green lettering appearing on the visor of the machine as it communicated a written message to the T-man. At her angle, Sabrina could not read it. Instead she looked back down to Orehem. A ribbon of sand was curled beside him, like something gossamer leaking out of his broken body. The wind stirred at her feet, and it was gone.

"Officer Pitt," the T-man said, turning from the L'ved.

"Yes," Pitt said, straightening.

"You indicated that you had searched and secured the scene."

"We did, we tended to the wounded and established a perimeter as soon as we arrived."

"How did this contraband necklace go unnoticed?"

Pitt's eyes darted before he answered. "My cadet must have missed it."

The L'ved shifted again.

Pitt continued, "The scene was chaotic when we arrived, and my cadet—"

"Is your responsibility," the T-man said before he turned to Sabrina. "Thank you, Cadet Sabryia, you are dismissed." Sabrina nodded, her mouth dry, and walked past Pitt. "You, too." The investigator added, looking at Pitt. "Essential personnel only."

ȧ

Her only ride back to the station was a cruiser shared with Pitt, Boyle, and Abner. They spread themselves and their gear out in the front seats, insisted there was no space left and suggested Sabrina ride in back, like a prisoner. She said nothing in response to the indignity and waited for the door to slide open.

Boyle pulled away abruptly before she could be seated, throwing her backwards with a thump. She wedged herself between the door and the corner of the seat in order to secure herself as Boyle broke one speed regulation after another.

Sabrina's headset vibrated and blinked in her lap. She turned the visor in her hands. A picture of Lindsey's face appeared. Her grin seemed to make her cheekbones even more pronounced, so sharp they defied belief. Her unruly hair had been pulled back although one lock had escaped and brushed against her temple and collar—a high green collar that brought out the green in her eyes and the regal sweep of her neck. Even in the back seat, with the screen up, Sabrina knew better than to take a personal call in front of Pitt and Boyle. She clutched the visor and hoped Lindsey would leave a message.

They circled around the base of Hill 37, its crown of fences glittering in the glare of flood lights. The cruiser rocked over a bump, and they headed down Condorcet Road.

A message had appeared on the visor with Lindsey's face beside it.

"Running late. Something came up at the community center."

Sabrina drew a keyboard in the air. With her visor on, the lettered keys floated in the air before her. She typed a response.

"Something old, or something new?"

Lindsey's response flickered in the air above the grid of the keyboard.

"Don't want to be around a crowd tonight. Don't want to suck down hydrocarbons either."

"Old then," Sabrina typed. "See you soon."

ɋ

Boyle turned down Stirner Avenue and stopped at the corner of Ingersoll Street to pick up his own cadet, Jacob. The three men upfront shuffled and rearranged their gear to make space for him. Through the glass prisoner screen she could overhear bits of their conversation.

"Who is the prisoner?"

"Cadet Sabryia."

Laughter, followed by more comments, too low for her to hear. Her temples began to throb, and it only grew worse as they pulled into the bright light of the station's vehicle bay. Pitt took his time collecting his things, greeting other officers finishing their shifts before he unlocked the latch allowing Sabrina to get out. As soon as the door was unlocked, she kicked it open so that Pitt had to catch it.

"Ride too bumpy for you?" Pitt asked.

Walk away. Walk away.

"Not as bad as the bump that occultist got, I suppose," Boyle added.

"At least I could keep up with him," Sabrina said snapping around, looking down at Pitt's gut. "Must be hard to pass the physical, hauling that extra weight around."

Off-duty officers gathered nearby laughed. "That is a senior officer you are speaking to," Boyle reminded her.

"*Senior* is right," Sabrina scoffed and stepped around them both.

"Cadet." Pitt yelled at her back. "One of these days you'll see how physical I can get."

ἀ

It was after the shift change, so Sabrina had the showers to herself. Not that the women's locker room was ever crowded … there were too few female officers for that. Even with the nearby Ministry of Public Welfare sharing the facility, the showers, sinks, and stalls had an abandoned, even dilapidated air. Most of the lockers sat empty. The floor mats remained dry, the benches unoccupied. The tiles were discolored from dust and grit, rather than mildew. The facilities were simply not used enough to build up the moisture for mold to flourish. Sabrina had placed her lock adjacent to a few lockers that the cleaning crews used, just so she did not feel so alone.

A solitary fan with rusted blades rotated in a window near the ceiling, its speed much too slow to move any air. Windows had been opened alongside to let the wind do what the fan could not. Sabrina actually preferred this. The feel of the ocean breeze on her skin after a shower reminded her of visits to the shore with Lindsey and the sense of freedom that came on those long days off from school.

She buried herself under a stream of hot water. Salt, grit, and blood washed off her and spun down the drain. More than grime, she knew she had to wash herself clean of the previous hours, the traumas, failures, and humiliations, especially before she saw Lindsey. It was *her* day, after all.

She closed her eyes and listened to the water drumming on her head. When the five-minute time limit had lapsed, she moved to the next showerhead, slapped the wall switch and continued. She tried to let the sound fill her mind, as if it could push out the images and feelings of the past shift. Her fingertips were pink raisins by the time she finished. The mirror inside the locker reflected her. In the soft overhead light, her naked body appeared blue. She studied the curve of her hips, the hollow of her waist—features she had wished so hard against as she was growing up, afraid that if she became too feminine she would not be able to compete with the boys and attain her dream of being an officer. To Lindsey's endless amusement, Sabrina had been horror struck at the appearance of her breasts, but as they had grown and settled into a modest size, she had been satisfied that they would not be in her way and were still large enough that they caught men's eyes. *Men's* eyes, not boys. She found boys her own age idiotic, but men who were a little older were tolerable. She had even come to appreciate the narrow cinch of her waist and the way a man's forearms could pass along its curve and wrap around her.

If she would ever let one close enough. She had met plenty at the academy, but as soon as they had realized she was opting for a position as a street officer and not in an administrative role, they had closed off to her, every last one—except for Sean.

At her locker, she put on clean clothes, stretching as she pulled a warm knit shirt over her head and stepped into a snug pair of trousers. They were soft and form fitting and a welcome change to the patrol suit.

She toweled her hair as dry as possible, deciding she would let the air do the rest. From inside the locker, she pulled out a necklace Lindsey had made for her. It was strung with large beads shaped like heads, each one with a different mood on its face. She rolled *confused* between her thumb, and forefinger, while the beads for *happy, sad, frightened, angry, sick, dead, cocky,* and *surprised* looked on. Each of their expressions wrought with lifelike detail.

She donned the necklace, then picked up her visor. She contemplated calling Sean but decided against it. He was probably resting. Instead, she tapped into the hospital interface and looked up his status. He was listed as stable. That was enough for her. She texted Lindsey.

She picked up her civilian shoes and laced them up, taking satisfaction in the pressure they created around her feet and the way the laces made perfectly symmetrical bows. She found her own roll pod in the parking deck below the station, a simple model with silver paneling and black interior. Her eyes performed a cursory inspection of the tires and the windscreen. At least no words were scratched into the paneling, or genitalia drawn on the windows with excrement. The tires were still inflated too. She whispered a silent thanks to the universe as she settled in and started the motor.

Her comcube was plugged into the pod's control panel. As she drove, she depressed a button on the wheel and scrolled through a number of names displayed on the screen. She highlighted the one she wanted. Sean answered.

"What did the doctors say?" she asked.

"I'll be fine, even back to work in three days."

"That's fast."

"Hard to keep a Lysander lad down." There was noise on the line as someone spoke to him in a chipper voice that Sabrina found irritating. She heard the rattle of a cart and the clank of a hospital tray as the nurse delivered Sean's meal, the noises were quickly followed by the shifting of bedclothes as Sean presumably sat up in bed. The chipper voice continued speaking in the background, much longer than necessary. Whoever this nurse was, she seemed to be striking up a conversation with Sean. Sabrina raised her voice to cut through.

"Glad to hear you are feeling better."

"Thanks," Sean said distractedly. Sabrina was not sure if it was directed towards her or the nurse. But when his voice started again, she knew she had recaptured his full attention. "What about you? I don't want that sicko to bother you. You have evals coming up."

"I'll be fine. I didn't get stabbed." Did a part of her wish she had been? At least a stab wound was something tangible, something that could be treated and could heal.

"It's all *crite,* you know that."

She bit her lip. "I know. You hear stories. You dismiss them. Then it happens to you."

"And for all the stories you hear of some strange coincidence—one of those freaks cursing an officer and then his blaster blowing up in his face or his suit failing—there are 50 others who get 'cursed' and nothing happens."

She felt a little better, but she was not sure if it was because of what he said or just the act of talking to him.

"What are you doing for fun now?" he asked.

"It's Lindsey's birthday. We're going up to Joseph and Magdalene's for dinner."

"That is just what you need, a trip up the Bay Road with the wind in your hair. Open the air vents, pop the top, play some music. Most of all have fun. That is a direct order from your supervisor."

"Yes sir."

"See you on Six-Day."

Chapter 5
Joseph and Magdalene's

Sabrina swerved to miss a man on a pedal bike as she pulled into the restaurant parking lot. Her haste was wasted. A look around revealed no sign of Lindsey's roll pod. This was late, even by Lindsey's standards.

A cool breeze off the ocean greeted Sabrina as she stepped out, the *kush-kush* of breakers and the squawk of sea birds filling her ears. The restaurant was a low, squat building made of plaster and earth with a timber roof. Square, wood-framed windows were open partway to allow in the fresh sea breeze. Smoke puffed out of the wide, stone chimney in the center of the building. A hanging wood sign with peeling paint squeaked in the wind. It read: JOSEPH AND MAGDALENE'S SEASIDE RESTAURANT. When Joseph spotted her in the doorway, he pulled himself up from a stool behind the counter, waddling a bit on stiff knees, a bright white smile under his bushy gray mustache. Sabrina moved to close the distance between them quickly, reluctant to make the old man walk any farther than necessary. He hugged her, patting her on her shoulders, but his smile faded quickly. "What's wrong?" he asked.

"Long day. Lindsey's late."

"She is always late," Joseph said leading her to their usual table outside on the patio. Sabrina forced a smile. Joseph was right, and it was Lindsey's night after all, but Sabrina had not realized how much she had wanted to see her friend, simply to put the rest of the day's events out of her mind.

The moon rose, a white marble rolling across a puddle of spilled ink. Sabrina had drained three pots of tea and watched the tables turn twice around her before she heard the faint jingle of the bells Lindsey had braided into her locks.

She was in a brown jacket that hugged her waist but opened up around her chest and neck revealing the smoothness of her brown skin. A blue blouse sparkled beneath the jacket with stones that Lindsey had sewn in herself. A red sash circled her waist in place of a belt. Her locks were pulled back into a ponytail tied with a ribbon that matched her sash.

Lindsey bounced on her toes at the sight of Sabrina, who sat with her arms folded. But before she could cross the patio, a couple seated at a table pulled Lindsey aside.

"Lindsey!" the woman cried. "We just love what you did with the mural on Ayers."

"It's even better than the one on Condorcet," the man said.

Lindsey put her hand to her breast, giving Sabrina the quickest of glances. "Thank you, the students worked very hard."

"Some of those colors though, they are amazing. Where did you get them?" the woman asked, reaching out to grab Lindsey's arm.

"Well, they are not actually ministry-approved," she said lowering her voice.

"I knew it!" the husband exclaimed.

"Oh, Lindsey, we're so tired of the ministry-issued colors," the woman said breathlessly. "We'd like to redo our own place but can't find any colors we like."

"Well, I make them myself."

The couple stared at one another agog.

"I use plants I grow on my balcony, stones, soil, shrubs from the desert. Even a coral or two from the sea if I can find them," Lindsey said.

The woman leaned forward, her face filled with the frisson of conspiracy, "We will pay you, handsomely, if you will redo our place. Magdalene said you did the interior of the restaurant. Is that true?"

"I did," she said, stealing another glance Sabrina's way. Sabrina kept her eyes fixed on the flagstone floor of the patio, tapping her foot.

"Fantastic. You have real talent," the husband said. "What are you going to do with it?"

As Lindsey began to explain that she was applying to the arts program down in Lysander, Sabrina pushed out her chair, walked past them, and jumped the patio wall. She landed on the soft sand of the beach. She was rounding the corner of the building, the parking lot in sight, when Lindsey called out her name.

Sabrina continued, jumping the wall of a second patio on the side of the building that was not yet opened for the season. Tables and chairs stood stacked in the corner under a tarpaulin. There was a bang and a rattle as Lindsey fought with the patio gate that Sabrina had so easily hurdled. When she could not get it to open, she simply climbed over and tumbled onto the sand.

"Sabrina, stop," she said trying her best to run over uneven ground.

Sabrina turned to look at her friend. Firelight lit her now—the glow from the bread oven. They were beside the kitchen where Magdalene was sliding loaves of bread in and out on a wood paddle. Lindsey's sash was askew. Her palms were chalky with stone dust, and her knees were sandy. One of her locks had come loose and dangled down her face so that a bell hung just below her lip. It tinkled as she brushed it aside. "Sabrina, I'm sorry."

"I've waited two hours, Lindsey. I know it's your birthday, but that's a long time. I'm about to piss myself from all the tea I drank. And then you stop and chat with Sam and Suzie Suck-up."

As the fires flared within the oven, Sabrina caught the liquid gleam of tears in Lindsey's eyes. It was her 19th birthday, but she seemed years younger. Sabrina could still see in her face the girl drawing pictures in the playground dust, saving beetles in her pockets.

"I'm sorry, Sabrina, I just wanted them to shut up, I did," she said wiping her eyes and shaking her head. "I just wanted to be with you. It's just been a long day."

Sabrina dropped down against one of the covered chairs, air hissing out from beneath the tarpaulin as she sat. "No, I'm sorry. I had a terrible day. Terrible. I wanted to just forget about it, and I guess I kind of dragged it along with me."

Lindsey tore the tarpaulin off another chair, dragged it over, and sat down next to Sabrina. "Want to talk about it."

"No."

"Me neither."

They both laughed. The sound brought Joseph out to the patio. Lindsey bounced up beside him. "Joseph, my dear, can we eat out here?"

ȁ

They stuffed themselves with crispy flat bread, topped with finely diced onions, peppers, and tomatoes drizzled in olive oil. The last customers cleared out of the back patio, and a few lingered on the beach where Joseph had one of his staff build a bonfire. Sabrina and Lindsey fell into a contented silence as they watched the silhouettes of children and their parents moving against the dancing light.

Magdalene cleared the empty platter. Joseph followed her inside. The foam on the waves breaking on the beach was ghostly white in the moonlight. The air had grown chilly. Lindsey unfolded the sash from around her waist and wrapped it about her shoulders. Joseph reappeared, Magdalene following him through the doorway as he carried a honey cake, his hand curled protectively around a single candle flickering in the wind.

Sabrina felt her heart skip a beat. She stood up, her chair falling to the floor behind her.

"Joseph! Where did you get that! It's contraband!"

Joseph and Magdalene wore identical expressions of children, caught by their parents.

"It is just a single candle," Joseph stammered. "We thought, for Lindsey's birthday it would be all right."

Lindsey wore a pleading look that said, *"But this is Joseph and Magdalene. . ."*

"Joseph, Magdalene, I have to arrest people for things like this," Sabrina said, that inverted sword lying on the bloody roadway flashing in her mind. She shuddered.

The couple looked over to them, their complexions soft and even, their eyes shining in the light of the candle. That light, it was almost like magic, Sabrina thought before a more stringent thought replaced it: there was a reason such things were outlawed. Superstition was intoxicating, just like the illegal brews sold out of the back of pharmacies.

Joseph bent to blow the candle out. In its flickering light, Sabrina could see the deep creases of a frown that had formed at the corners of Lindsey's mouth.

"Wait," Sabrina said, raising her hand. "I'll let you off with a warning. But I can't do it next time."

Magdalene smiled and clasped her hands together. "We're too old to be criminals," she said as her husband placed the cake and two smaller plates in front of Lindsey.

When they were alone again, Lindsey carefully lifted the candle out of the soft cake, turned it so that the wax dripped on one of the smaller plates, then stuck the candle in the cooling wax, fixing it in place.

"It is like you've handled a candle before, Lindsey," Sabrina said.

"You know me, I'm a law breaker."

"Well, since we are already breaking the law, should we do the annual prediction?"

Lindsey smiled conspiratorially, her chair creaking as she leaned forward. "I knew you would ask."

"It's a birthday tradition and a much better one I might add, no evidence," Sabrina said gesturing to the candle.

"It's so sweet. I wonder where they got it."

"Who knows? We find contraband all the time. If it were anyone else besides Magdalene and Joseph, I'd say it was pretty sick."

"Stop it," Lindsey said, slapping the table. She shook her head as if warding off a chill and her smile returned. "Sorry, it's just that they are our friends."

"I know. I'm sorry. It's not like they are occultists or something."

Lindsey was quiet a long while, staring into the candle for such an extended period of time that Sabrina was about to ask if something was wrong when she looked up and said, "I did not take my medication all week."

"I am off duty."

"Now who is the law breaker?" Lindsey said with a sly smile. She placed her elbows on the table and leaned forward, closing her eyes and touching her fingers to her temples. The sound of the kitchen seemed to recede, the movement of the wind and sea growing to fill the void. "What do we want to know?" she whispered.

"By this time next year, will we both be in universities of our choice?"

"By this time next year will either of us have boyfriends?"

"Lindsey!"

Lindsey's eyes snapped open. "Or should I just ask if Sabrina will get laid."

"Stop it!" Sabrina slapped her forearm, but that did nothing to quell Lindsey's laughter. "Come on, let's get serious. You have my question."

"All right. All right." Lindsey settled back into position over the candle. She grew still before opening her eyes again. "You want me to ask about Sean."

She was not joking. Sabrina's mind spun. She had not even told Lindsey about her day, preferring not to lay such a burden on her friend on her birthday. Lindsey had no idea about Sean's injury, so Sabrina wondered what she could mean. Before she could think much longer, she replied, as coolly as she could, "No, you have my question."

Lindsey nodded and closed her eyes again. The candle flickered and the wind chimes twirled and sang. She settled into a gentle rocking motion on her elbows, her face peaceful and serene as she moved into the space where she saw her visions. A drip of wax formed like a tear on the tip of the candle and rolled down its length to disappear into a spreading pool. The sea breeze moved the corners of the folded tarpaulins and caused one of Lindsey's bells to chime. The wind carried the sound of the children playing about the fire. Without warning, Lindsey jerked, kicking the table and sliding forward as if fainting. The plates clanged, and the candle fell over and died. Lindsey gasped as if struck and began to slide from her chair.

"Lindsey!" Sabrina said, "What's wrong?"

"I didn't— I don't—"

Sabrina rushed around the table, putting her hands on Lindsey's shoulders. "It's all right. I'm here." She clasped Lindsey's hand. It was cold as if all the blood had rushed out of it. Lindsey's body was trembling, and her chest heaved like a sprinter just off the track.

"I'll call Magdalene," Sabrina said.

"No, no," Lindsey said, straightening herself in her chair. "Maybe I just did not stop the medication soon enough. "

"What happened?"

"I don't know," she said, looking at the fallen candle. "I did not see … anything. Nothing. Then I just kept trying, like trying to force it. Then it was just like this big black …nothingness came down on me. Like a blanket wrapped around me while I was under the sea, struggling to move, but sinking, in darkness, emptiness. No air. No breath. Like death." She pulled the scarf up more tightly around her shoulders, her face full of fear. "Do you think I've lost the ability to see visions, to predict completely? That I've been on the drugs so long—"

Sabrina was unsure what to say, knowing that as a cadet, and eventually an officer, she had often hoped that Lindsey's condition would go away naturally. But seeing the heartbreak in Lindsey's face, Sabrina hated herself for wishing it.

"I'm sure that's what it is," Sabrina said. "You just should have stopped the drugs sooner. You never lose something like that."

Lindsey did not reply. She seemed transfixed by the candle. Sabrina stared too. The string of smoke rising up from it curled away in a breeze that felt colder. It brought to mind the curling ribbon of sand that had stretched out and disappeared beside Orehem's body. Sabrina shuddered and pushed the image out of her mind. "You want some water?" she asked.

"Yes."

Sabrina went to the kitchen. When she returned with a full carafe a few moments later, Lindsey's expression was flat and mournful. By the tracks on her cheeks, Sabrina could see she had been crying. Guilt was welling up inside her for asking for her to make a prediction in the first place.

"Can we walk on the beach?" Lindsey asked.

They removed their shoes and stepped off the patio into the sand. They walked in silence for a long distance before they turned around, facing the restaurant and the bonfire that still leapt up at the night sky. Lindsey had the look of someone trying to shake a bad dream. "Let's build a sand castle," she suggested.

The logs of the fire settled into a steady smolder. Parents wrapped themselves in blankets as their children joined Sabrina and Lindsey as they constructed castle walls, turrets, and a keep. It was not the most lavish of castles, since they only had broken seashells and sticks to work with as tools, but Lindsey's skill showed through. Soon there were windows, eves, and parapets complete with merlons and crenels.

"A shining city on a hill," Lindsey said in her best mockery of one of Sabrina's uncle D'Agosta's old audiocom addresses. She stood back from their finished work and held her broken shell over her head. They burst out laughing.

They wrapped their arms about one another as they walked to the parking lot. Lindsey's purple CRP, or "the bean" as she called it, was beside Sabrina's. Lindsey lifted the windscreen to the roll pod then halted, holding the half-sphere up over her head. "Sabrina, I don't want to be alone tonight."

"No problem," Sabrina said. "I'll follow you home." She trailed Lindsey north on the Bay Road as the lights of the city shimmered over the water and the crowns of the hills moved closer. Lindsey drove like an old woman, slow and careful like always. It took an effort on Sabrina's part not to follow too closely.

She glanced up as a flood light flared on the side of Hill 34. For an instant she could catch the glint of fences and razor mesh. She was too far away to see the intruder, but she could follow his path as one light went out and another blazed. By now she knew that a pair of cadets was already likely descending upon the unfortunate scrit. From her last time on duty, after processing her own prisoner, she had checked the records from the past three years. Incidences of scrits on the hills had risen, just like the reports of code violations and violence in the cities. The thought made her stomach queasy. But her uncle D'Agosta had not betrayed any worry and so she resolved that she wouldn't either.

Sabrina parked beside Lindsey in the parking deck and followed her up the bland and empty stairwell to the seventh floor. The building was ministry designed, standard in its layout and identical to Sabrina's own apartment building but for the doors which were decorated uniquely by each resident. The walls were blank but for cracks and a sign indicating which days reclamation materials could be set outside. Another sign listed names of residents and which days they were assigned community duties. Lindsey Medhina was the only name written in purple glitter ink.

Lindsey's keys jangled in the lock. The inside of her apartment was a welcome contrast to the corridor. A sea breeze wafted through the open windows and gently filled the curtains. The sterile smell of concrete and construction resin was replaced by the scent of earthen pots and the pheasant eyes, hollyhocks, and anemone that grew on the balcony. Like her murals, Lindsey's apartment was painted in non-standard colors, the bedroom in soft sky blues, the kitchen alcove in warm earth tones, and the sitting area a welcoming cheery orange. Only her work space near the window was white, but this had more to do with light. An easel with a mess of paints on its tray stood near the window. A number of sculptures in various stages of completion stood nearby. The artwork migrated around the room from there, paintings adorned walls, figurines perched on table tops, tapestries hung from door frames leading into the hallway, the bedroom, and the kitchen.

As always, Sabrina took it all in slowly, savoring the vivid feel. Lindsey seemed too tired or too accustomed to her work to take notice. She disappeared into the bathroom, ran the water then reemerged in pajamas. After rearranging the cushions on the couch and pulling out its sleeping mattress, she dropped down onto it, flicking on the view screen.

Sabrina went to the bathroom to wash her face. She took her time examining the octopus Lindsey had painted into the corner of the wall. By using the perspective of the converging surfaces, she had created the illusion that the octopus was reaching out towards the viewer. The illusion made her slightly dizzy as she brushed her teeth with the toothbrush she kept under Lindsey's sink.

They sat in bed, each curled under a blanket, facing the video panel. Lindsey did not last five minutes. Her soft rhythmic breathing told Sabrina that she was sound asleep and would not wake until morning— just as it had been since they were little. It always took longer for Sabrina's body to find the relaxation required for sleep.

A picture frame sat on the table beside the couch. Sleek, silver, and simple, it was a stark contrast to the rest of the apartment. This was intended. Sabrina had given it to Lindsey a year earlier. It was supposed to represent Sabrina's own taste, while Lindsey had given her the same picture in a frame that reflected her own distinct style. The picture showed Lindsey, her parents, her brother Sam, and Sabrina at the beach.

Sam was still a boy, and Lindsey and Sabrina still had the bodies of girls under their swimsuits.

Lindsey's family had been Sabrina's refuge of normalcy growing up, an escape from the institutional grounds of the Head Ministry. Her uncle D'Agosta had been unendingly kind and generous to her, but despite his generosity and his power, there were things he could not do, like take her to the beach or the market. He was the Head Minister, tasked with governing their world within the walls. Their protector. Their savior. It would not do for him to appear at the beach in swim trunks. She knew more than others how the Head Ministry was a prison to him.

But Lindsey and her parents, under a shroud of normalcy, could take her such places. It was with them that she made her first visit to the market. She had accompanied D'Agosta on inspection trips to the farms south of the city where their food was produced, but he never took her to the loud, bustling, colorful markets where buyers and sellers haggled over prices.

Why he had granted Sabrina such beneficence above other orphans she would never know and did not question out of some fear he might reconsider and the spell might be broken. He had saved her from a tragic life. Both her parents had been killed in a traffic accident. She had no memory of it, thankfully. There was no pain of loss that way. She did not even know their names. Her earliest memory did not even include them: she was four and D'Agosta, holding her in his arms, was on what must have been one of her first tours of the Head Ministry building. They were standing before a shining silver orb floating within a glass column. He had only taken her there once and she had never seen it again. Yet the memory persisted.

She turned her attention to the view panel. The vids at this time of night were all from before the Cataclysm and the Transition—as if only in the dead of night could the ghosts of the past reemerge. Sabrina flicked through vids of old pitchball matches, animated shows, and nature documentaries. The vids had been screened and censured to eliminate inappropriate references to nations, faiths, or beliefs. But, to a careful watcher, they still revealed secrets and, being an insomniac, Sabrina had become an expert at finding references the censors had missed on the late-night vids.

Late one night, Sabrina had seen a vid of a pitchball match in which a player, after scoring, had looked up and made a motion as if sending kisses skyward. Sabrina had recoiled in revulsion and told her uncle immediately the next morning. He gravely explained to her that such hideous expressions were once common, even during public events. Sabrina never saw the vid played again.

The nature docus revealed to her what the planet had looked like one hundred years ago, before the radioactive fires had scorched its face. There had been green forests, seas of waving grass, and high mountains—not like the dusty hills of Fortinbras—but towering masses with jagged black peaks and rivers of snow, *snow,* flowing down them in currents that moved like stone, just inches at a time.

It made her sad to think that all these places had been made inhospitable now to biological life, all by faiths that claimed to cherish the very planet they had destroyed.

She felt herself beginning to drift by the third vid, one where colorful girl-heroes flew through the air to fight forces of unquestionable evil. She closed her eyes to the sound of their high-pitched voices accompanied by explosions and the cries of their enemies.

In sleep, she went to that place almost all her dreams inevitably led her: a pink room with white curtains moving in the breeze. She heard the sound of a siren. Her eyes were fixed on a painting, a sailboat in a wide open sea. If she looked to her right, she would see blue forget-me-nots on the windowsill, but she could never make herself look in that direction, despite the many times she had been in this room in countless dreams.

Then the room was gone. She was somewhere else, standing before that polished silver orb, D'Agosta's warm, gravelly voice filling her ear. "This is our failsafe, our last salvation." His voice seemed to catch. "A solution that is final."

A blood-red face in the sun. "Into your weapons I send my—"

She snapped awake. Her skin was wet with sweat, and her heart pounded in her chest. Her comcube was buzzing on the table beside her. She slapped it then opened the view screen.

It was a message from D'Agosta. Apparently he was having trouble sleeping as well.

`Come see me. First thing in the morning. Anything else can wait.`

She rolled over to check on Lindsey. She was still sound asleep. Sabrina slipped out of bed and put her shoes back on, her fingers threading the laces slowly as her heart beat settled. The sun would not rise for another two hours. She knew she would not be able to get back to sleep. In the kitchen, fanciful creatures with antennae, horns, and wings, stared at her as she drank a glass of water. They were Lindsey's ceramic pill jars, their ridiculous appearance a cover for the seriousness of the prescriptions they contained.

She drank as unanswered questions hung in her mind regarding which schools they would be accepted into, where they would be living in a year, how many more birthdays they would share together.

She put down the glass quietly. Worry was a wasted emotion—at least that was what her uncle had told her. She went to the door and closed it softly behind her.

"Happy birthday, my friend. Here's to many more."

Chapter 6

Angelo D'Agosta

"Identify yourself." The ministry guard swiveled the wall gun towards Sabrina.

The gun was ancient—it still used chemically propelled projectiles—and it sat on a groaning, rotating mount at the top of one of the ministry towers. Long belts of bullets, their casings gleaming in the morning sun, looped down the side and folded over themselves at the guard's booted feet.

Sabrina said nothing. Instead she watched as the guard turned his head to the display panel beside him. Pheromone sniffers on either side of the gate had already confirmed Sabrina's security clearance. He waved his hand, and the blast doors began to automatically open.

The doors, like the guns, were artifacts. They had never been attacked by conventional means. Instead sun, sea, salt, had been allowed to assault them, turning them the color rust. In the light of the rising sun, they looked as if they had been painted in blood.

They opened and revealed a different world.

Pear and pomelo trees swayed in the breeze over grass so thoroughly manicured that not a single leaf or fruit rested on the ground. A fountain in the center of the garden caught the sun's rays, the water streaming outwards in sparkling channels to more rows of trees. Only the black shadow of the audiocomm tower rising from the north wing of the Head Ministry broke the symmetry of the garden.

Sabrina took a deep breath, inhaling the scents of fruit blossoms that mixed with a breeze that carried hints of the sea.

VOLUME I – THE CITY

The smell of her home.

She walked up the path through the dappled sunlight and approached a tour group of school children. Their teachers watched from nearby as they used the great stone faces placed at intervals throughout the garden as climbing gyms. Each face had a long flat nose, small pursed mouths, and narrow slits for eyes. Sabrina had been little when the eccentric art pieces had been installed. Her uncle had called them his "Fallen Gods" and had lifted her up so she could play on them. Not quite metal, not quite stone, they emitted a faint humming sound and were always warm to the touch. Sabrina had never been able to shake a certain animal wariness of them. But these children had, their rubber shoes and sticky hands scrambling for purchase over a nostril, an eye, a lip.

She passed through a final gauntlet of the heads, set on either side of the stone footpath and entered the Rotunda. A tour guide was leading a group of older children through the circular colonnade.

"The Rotunda is made from glass and transparent poly-ethylene composite bricks," the female guide explained. "These materials were chosen to reinforce the values of clarity and transparency by which the Founders envisioned government must abide. Even the clock you see over the main entrance was made without sides in order to reveal its inner workings. The Founders also designed the Rotunda so that no matter where the sun tracks, no matter the time of year, there is light that shines on the Nine Founding Principles."

The children turned their faces upwards to the nine precepts laser-incised into the marble frieze just beneath the dome. The lettering was efficient and precise, not unlike the displays on Sabrina's visor: neat, clean, free of flourishes and seraphs. A scattering of rainbows and white sunlight danced across the letters, reflected by the pool of water set beneath the oculus of the dome.

Their teacher interrupted, asking the children to recite the principles from memory. In a droning group voice, they obeyed.

> *It is the absolutism of theism, its pernicious influence upon humanity, its paralyzing effect upon thought and action, that we must fight with all our power.*

> *All religions are versions of the same untruth, and the influence of religion and the effect of religious belief are always harmful.*

> *All religions, with their gods, their demi-gods, and their prophets, their messiahs and their saints, were created by the prejudiced fancy of men who had not attained the full development and full possession of their faculties.*

> *There is but one law for all, namely, that law which governs all law, the law of humanity, justice, equity—the law of nature and of nations.*

> *Law is the perfection of reason.*

> *The law is the point at which savagery ended because civilization stood in its path.*

VOLUME I – THE CITY

*Justice is immortal, eternal, and immutable, and the
development of law is only then a progress when it is
directed towards those principles which are eternal.*

*Nobody has a greater obligation to obey the law than
those who make the law.*

*Laws without arms would give us not liberty, but
licentiousness; and arms without laws, would produce
not subjection, but slavery.*

The tour guide led the children to another wing, promising to
show them the technology laboratories. Their voices died off, like
whispers in a crypt.

Sabrina made her way to the North Wing and her uncle's office.
After passing through a series of empty halls, her footsteps echoing off
cold marble, she stopped before two wooden doors, reaching to the
ceiling. Behind them the council members, the heads of the nine
ministries, would be seated around a table, their assistants lining the
walls. Sabrina turned to a smaller, adjacent door made of blond wood
and placed her hand on the knob.

The surface read the biochemical signature of her skin, a warm
tingle brushing across her palm. The pheromone sniffers on the lintel
hissed with an intake of air to re-confirm her identity. The door
unlocked. On the other side, a musty smelling carpet with explosions of
fading color and intricate mandala designs did battle with the gray on
white austerity of the building interior. The rug was allied with the rows
of ancient leather bound books set in glass shelves. The smooth,

machine-polished wood frames supporting the shelves appeared to have taken a neutral stance in the struggle between old and new. Most of the books were from before the Transition. They were outlawed outside of this room. D'Agosta explained that he kept them there for reference only.

An antique lamp stand stood in the corner in a glass case illuminated by the warm glow of recessed lights. Sabrina was not even sure it still functioned, but she assumed D'Ag kept it for some sentimental reason. Beside the lamp sat a small hunched man in a white lab coat with gray, fraying sleeves. His hair was a sagging bush of yellow-white that matched his mustache. In his hands, slightly misshapen from being double jointed, he held a screw driver which he used to secure the casing of what looked like a blaster.

"Moshi!" Sabrina cried.

The old man looked up, startled for a moment then smiled. "Sabrina, you are just in time to help me. Here, hold this."

She held the barrel of the blaster firm while Moshi twisted the screws into place. When he was finished, he lifted the gun up and aimed down the barrel.

"A new gun?"

"Well, it is that," he said. "A rail gun. It uses electromagnetic force to propel this." He dug into his pocket and produced what looked to be a small ball bearing. "Fire a stream of these, and you can cut through cement like it was wet bread. We can disassemble those old buildings along the Bay Road and use the pieces for new construction in weeks, instead of months." He lifted a magazine of the projectiles and showed where it clipped into the frame of the gun.

"You will have to build a few more cranes just to keep up," Sabrina said.

"Ah hah!" Moshi said, his eyebrows rising on his forehead. "We will not, because we have this!" He pulled a glittering suit from where it rested across the back of a chair, the thousands of small blue-black plates on its surface gleaming with an iridescent sheen. It was fresh from the laboratories. An experiment card still hanging to it read: `Prototype 11.1.12-9`.

As she held it, Sabrina was struck by its lightness and the way its material moved fluidly through her fingers.

"It's an amplification suit," Moshi explained. "If we're going to be cutting up giant slabs of concrete, we'll have to be able to pick them up—without a crane. I made it in your size."

"You didn't!"

"Of course I did," he chuckled. "You wore the first of the climbing suits. I still remember when you were just nine, that day you surprised D'Ag by climbing up the side of the ministry wall like a little gecko."

Sabrina remembered that day too, the exhilaration of climbing up the wall with such ease, how her uncle and Moshi shrank so small below her, their hands raised to their eyes to block the sun as she reached the top and stood up where she could see the sea spreading out to the eastern horizon.

"I can't imagine what this could do for us on patrol," she said handling the iridescent folds of the amplification suit. As soon as she said the words, she regretted them, as a dark shadow passed over

Moshi's features. He sat back down heavily, staring now at Sabrina's patrol suit, which she wished she could cover up.

"I build for peaceful purposes," Moshi said, disgusted. "It's your uncle who always seems to find a martial use of my inventions."

Sabrina knelt down on the floor beside him as she had done so many times. The only other fulltime resident of the ministry, Moshi had been an uncle to her as much as D'Ag. It was from him she had learned math, and it was Moshi who had provided needed levity, building her bouncing balls, elastic slings, and robotic grasshoppers that she would set loose in D'Ag's study.

"But Moshi, a person can't wake up and pass through the day without using your inventions. Fuel cells, light strips, heating ovens, communication cubes, water purification systems … the Twin Cities exist as much because of you as D'Ag and his council."

He let out a sigh, tapped the head of his screw driver on the chair arm then pointed at her suit. "I never meant for the climbing suits to be turned into—combat suits."

Sabrina cast her eyes to the floor. She noticed his shoes were untied.

"Moshi, when was the last time you left the ministry?"

He rubbed his temples before smoothing his mane of hair out over his scalp. "I don't quite remember, little sparrow. You see, I have trouble remembering things now-a-days."

"Take a break. Go for a trip through the cities. You'll see how your inventions make people's lives better."

"If your uncle will allow me. I came here this morning to show him these. They should earn me some time off."

"You've already earned it, Moshi. Everyone knows it but you. Even this morning the tour guides were leading children to see your labs."

He stood up suddenly. "Oh, dear. I am late. I was supposed to speak to them."

"Wait." Sabrina tugged him over to her by his jacket. She buttoned his collar down where he had forgotten then tied his shoes. He mumbled an embarrassed excuse about forgetting.

"You just have other things you have been thinking about," she said. "Now go blow those children's minds."

ἀ

She entered the next room, quietly, for this was D'Ag's formal office, and he had left its door to the council chamber open. Voices echoed and carried. She could hear as clearly as if she were seated at the council table. Two comfortable plush chairs waited invitingly before her uncle's desk, but she avoided them, aware that the squish of their cushions would give her away. Instead, she leaned against his desk.

Two framed pictures stared at her. One was of herself, much younger, standing along the seashore, a stick raised in her hand— undoubtedly a sword in her young imagination. The second was of a woman with olive skin. Short dark hair cut almost like a boy except for the long bangs hung across her face. The woman was Sabrina's only companion on the empty expanse of frosted glass that made the desk's surface. D'Ag had never revealed who she was or how he had known her.

She heard her uncle's voice. His diction was clipped and precise, like a scientist reading off a checklist. But the voice was also deep, honed from years of giving speeches over the audiocom. It was the voice of a man used to addressing thousands. She pictured him seated now, his chin resting on his fingers, as he and the ministers discussed the brawls that had erupted at the recent pitchball matches.

"Athletic pursuits are ritualistic violence," her uncle said. "It is no wonder that it spills over."

The security minister assured her uncle that additional officers could provide added security.

"But it is more than that. It is the way the players are beginning to be viewed," her uncle said.

"Like celebrities?" one minister said.

"Like gods," her uncle replied.

"We've put a stop to that," another minister said. "We have relocated them. They live among the mainstream population. It is clear they are part of the people, not set apart."

"Standing in a stadium with thousands calling your name sets you apart, no matter where you live," D'Ag said. "I've seen those heinous murals people paint of the players on the sides of houses."

Fans had created large colorful portraits of pitchball players that were dangerously rendered to make them look god-like. They were adorned with halos, lightning bolts, and glowing clouds. Most had been removed and replaced with murals painted by neighborhood youth with art students, like Lindsey, supervising. Another minister said she had passed by a strikingly beautiful mural on Holbach Street. There were murmurs of ascent. Sabrina touched her knuckle to her mouth. It was one of Lindsey's.

"Are these games worth the trouble?" her uncle asked, returning to the subject at hand.

"We can't ignore the other benefits that come from the pitchball matches," a minister replied.

"Atavistic screaming, curses, and people generally acting like beasts," her uncle said sourly.

"No, entertainment, recreation, distraction," a voice insisted.

"Unity and outlet for aggression," another voice for the games added.

There was a long silence before D'Ag relented. "I would have them do something more, enlightened, but I recognize the games are a release valve. But a valve must be controlled, lest it overflow. Commandant March, can you have more officers on patrol in the stands at the games?"

"Certainly," Commandant March, the head of security and station chief, replied. Sabrina swallowed. She realized she was eavesdropping on a superior officer. When she was a child, her practice of listening to her uncle's meetings had been educational. But as a cadet, she realized she might have to reconsider.

"Done. If there is no other business, my next appointment has arrived."

Shuffling noises and the murmur of casual conversations drifted in through the doorway as the council dispersed. Sabrina performed a quick survey of her uniform, ensuring every strap, buckle, and insignia was in place. D'Ag entered sweeping the tail of his jacket around him like a robe. His head was completely bald but for a crown of silver that rested behind his ears and encircled the back of his head. He embraced her and kissed her cheek, then settled into the high-backed chair behind his desk, picking up a data tablet waiting for him. While thumbing through its screen, he gestured to one of the thick-cushioned chairs before him. Sabrina, aware of how deep they were, was reluctant to settle into one. She would not be able to sit in it without leaning back too far and appearing to be "at ease," a pose she was reluctant to strike while in uniform. Instead, she settled on the arm of the chair.

D'Ag sighed loudly, looked up from his tablet. "If the arm of the chair was for sitting it would be called a seat, not an arm, would it not?" His eyes returned to the tablet, scanning its face back and forth for a few more moments, ignoring her. She said nothing but twisted her lips into a frown before crashing down into the chair harder and less gracefully than she had intended. Immediately, she felt like a little girl on an oversized sofa.

D'Agosta remained preoccupied until he tossed the tablet onto his desk with a growl.

"Poor results," he said. He explained how he and the education minister had picked a school with good community cohesion and put half the children in red uniforms and half in blue. Previous to the change, children saw themselves and their school as unified. They viewed those around them as talented, smart, affable. People you would want to befriend.

"Within three months, they had split," he said. "Children in red uniforms spend more time with other children in red uniforms, and blues do the same with blues. The uniforms are arbitrary. Yet now the students regard children in the other colors as not as trustworthy or smart and their own color as better." The muscles in D'Agosta's jaw flexed as his eyes fixated on a point in the corner of the room. "It's in us, Sabrina, lying there dormant, just waiting to be awoken, this hatred of 'the other.'"

The door opened, and his assistant Roslyn brought in a tray of tea and cookies. Sabrina struggled against the cushions of her chair, attempting to straighten herself. D'Ag took his cup and placed Sabrina's on the edge of the desk where she could reach it.

"So," he said after Roslyn had left. "Would you be willing to work on seventh day, patrolling a pitchball match?"

"Of course."

"Are you answering as a cadet or as a sports enthusiast?"

He knew her love of sports. The simplicity of a match. The physical challenge. But she also knew exactly how to reply.

"As a cadet. That is my focus now."

"Even though you would rather watch the game than have your back turned to it."

"I would rather uphold the law. You have said law is all that binds us together."

His eyes darted to the tablet he had discarded. "It is." He sipped from his tea and raised his head. "From everything I hear, you are becoming a fine cadet."

And she knew he *heard* much, from official reports to informal networks. She did not like the way he said "cadet" and, by his tone, she already knew what was coming next.

"You still do not want to consider applying to the law program?"

Pouring over law texts, memorizing arcane laws, spending her life behind a desk in a ministry building … each notion made her stomach knot tighter than the last. She picked up her tea cup weighing and weighed her response carefully. "The study of justice does interest me, sir. But I would rather gain knowledge from experience for a few years before I pursue that degree. Plus, I have not studied at all for those entrance exams."

"I could have that requirement waved."

"That would not be fair."

"I knew you would say that. Good."

"Officers are the foot soldiers of law and justice. Practical experience will enhance my formal studies."

He nodded, sipped his tea again. "On another note, I read the report from last night."

Sabrina hid her face behind her cup as she took a sip, willing herself to appear calm. She only pretended to drink. Her throat was too tight to swallow. The cup shook as she placed it back in the saucer. D'Ag was wearing his scientist's gaze now. This was the real reason he had summoned her.

"Why did you pursue the occultist alone?"

"Sean ordered me to, and I followed his guidance."

"Officer Maher, you mean."

"Yes, Officer Maher." Her fingernails dug into the soft surface of the chair.

"He was injured and could not accompany you. He must have known this."

"Perhaps he did not realize the extent of his injuries and planned to catch up with me. But I cannot report on what was going on in his head. "

"You just did."

Sabrina was aware she was trying to protect Sean, but her efforts were failing. She felt pinheads of sweat form on her back.

"Officer Maher was flagrantly violating regulations," D'Agosta continued.

"We were afraid the suspect might escape," she said. "We were closest to him, and we knew he must be hiding something."

"A half-truth. Your colleagues were likely to catch him. An injured officer brings the whole corps down."

"The whole corps would kill him." No reason to hide it, D'Ag had to know it already. "We wanted him alive."

D'Ag leaned back in his chair, rocking slightly. Behind him, the tops of the ancient city appeared against the blue of the sea. The city was old even in the time of the Cataclysm, and it was the only remnant of the old world that D'Ag or any head minister before him had not razed. Entry was forbidden, except for her uncle, of course. He had taken her many times as a girl. Her memories of running through the dusty, empty streets were some of her favorites.

"You've always been fascinated by the occultists," he said turning in his chair. At that moment the door opened again, and one of the T-men entered. He was adorned in formal ministry wear, a beige jacket over a plain white shirt. His helmet was a matching beige. Unspeaking, he set a case on the table, then exited.

D'Agosta ignored the intrusion. "You've asked questions about the occultists since you were little. I worry now that I provided too many candid answers, that I failed to instill the proper amount of fear in you."

She searched her feelings, her head feeling light with a surge of frustration that she often experienced when she was losing ground with him. She had learned that the truth was often the best way to disarm him.

"I was angry, Uncle. If anything I wanted to hurt the man myself. He tried to kill Sean—Officer Maher. But I realized bringing him in alive was the *just* thing to do." She could have stopped there but she continued. "If you want me to say I pursued him for more than that, I won't. I did not even know he was an occultist at that point." That lurid face in the sun. Those words, *Into your weapons*—"It surprised me as much as anyone else."

"The whole truth." He said, satisfied, and retreated, turning his attention to the T-man who had re-entered holding a syringe. Sabrina could not see his face, and he did not turn it to greet her as he prepared her uncle's arm for puncture with astringent wipes. "Forgive me, Sabrina, if I pry. You know I treasure honesty more than anything else and honesty begins with the self."

"Yes, sir. I appreciate it. I question myself all the time."

"Good."

The T-man removed the cap from the needle and pressed it into her uncle's arm. He did not wince.

"You are becoming more woman than girl, more cadet than child. I am pleased. Would you like a cookie?" he said, pointing to the plate with his chin.

"No, thank you."

"Officer Maher's reports are very positive on your performance."

"Thank you, sir …"

"Officers Pitt and Boyle are not, however."

Blood began to flow into a vial in the T-man's hand.

Eager to counter, Sabrina shrugged. "There are politics even in the station. I am most concerned with my direct supervisor's appraisals." She nodded towards the T-man. "Uncle, shouldn't you let the nurses do that? They are trained. The one I go to for my monthly donation does it painlessly."

If the T-man heard her, he did not acknowledge it.

"Apparently, they believe I am too important." D'Agosta smiled, also not acknowledging the man taking his blood. One vial was filled already. "But let it not be said that I won't bleed for my cities."

"Of course," Sabrina said. She finished her tea and reached to place the cup on the desk in preparation to leave.

As if to capture her with his words, D'Agosta spoke. "Sabrina, I do not want you following up on this case. Officer Maher can do it alone. You are removed."

She felt a vacuum in her chest. A dozen questions came to mind and faded as she anticipated his answers: *On whose authority?* D'Agosta's. *For what reason?* He owed her none. *What did he know of how this would affect her?* Nothing—he didn't care. Everything—he was trying to sabotage her. She stood, clenching her fists, staring at the empty teacup. One question surfaced over the others.

"On what grounds?" She said the words slowly, one by one.

"That it is dangerous and potentially upsetting. Pitt and Boyle both said you appeared visibly shaken at the scene of the man's death. 'Weak' and 'Emotionally frail' were the words they used, I believe."

She could not bear to look at him, or the impervious T-man, his helmet obscuring his face as he stared at the thick blood tricking out of her uncle's vein. Outside, the sun darkened as if a cloud had passed before it. A shadow fell across the sea and the old city. Her temples pounded.

"This is my job. I have to become used to such scenes. The only way is through exposure."

"You were exposed," D'Ag said. The T-man switched to another vial. "And you will be exposed again, I am sure. The process should be gradual, else you burn out. I am thinking of your career more than you give me credit for."

She was silent.

"You disagree?" he asked.

"May I be frank?"

"Of course."

"Are you making this decision as my uncle or Head Minister?"

"It should not matter to you."

She began to pace, breathing deeply, a technique he had taught her in order to master her own emotions. But before she could speak, the door chimed and a second T-man walked in, followed by two more, typing furiously on their data tablets.

"Good morning sir, Notorn Corporation—" D'Agosta silenced him with a wave of his hand. He stopped and seemed to notice Sabrina for the first time, even though he was nearly on top of her. She rolled her eyes. The helmets and the way they obscured peripheral vision were simply ridiculous. She suddenly had no patience for them or her uncle or any of his lackeys. She moved to leave.

"You will be assigned scrit duty until further notice," D'Agosta said.

Sabrina gave as shallow a bow as she dared. "Good day, minister."

She seethed all the way down the hallway. D'Ag was gracious when it suited him, but intrusive and disrespectful of all things he deemed lowly or base—of course those lowly things were always the things she found most important. She wondered if he thought her interest in being an officer was just a passing fancy, a game, her uniform a costume to be played in the same way that she had played with a stick as her sword years ago. She realized she had made a mistake coming there that morning. Meeting in the place where she had grown up shifted the advantage to him. *Let him come to me next time,* she thought. Fortibras was her city, after all. Even if D'Ag governed it, he was no longer *of* it, isolated here in his marble castle across the bay. What did he know of the realities in the station or the streets or of being a woman?

She stopped in the Rotunda. Her pulse was pounding. Each tick of the mechanical clock echoed loudly in the emptiness.

Chapter 7

Scrit

The lights of Fortinbras twinkled below Sabrina as the rocky ground of Hill 36 crunched underfoot. An ocean breeze bent the stems of a patch of hyssop, scattering the minty scent of their leaves. Her side of the hill was empty, the sentry lights slumbered as the only movement around them was the occasional field mouse or bat, swooping low to catch a meal. Sabrina sat down, her hands resting on her knees, and cycled through a series of menus displayed on her visor, flipping through them with quick snapping motions of her wrist. It was against protocol while on duty, but she clicked into the station's database to see how cases had been assigned. She found what she wanted, closed all the menus and called Lindsey.

"Slow night on the hill?"

"Like you wouldn't believe."

"No scrits?"

"Not a single one. Wouldn't mind the target practice."

"Stop it. I always feel so sorry for them. Are their brains really wasted?"

"They usually have no short-term memory. No one knows what the occultists do to them to make them that way. The one thing they do remember is that they want to find some piece of the old temple."

The line was quiet.

"Lindsey, you there."

"Yeah, just thinking about the scrits. It's sad. If D'Ag really wanted to put a stop to it, he could just pave over the whole hill."

"He'd like to, but we don't have the materials—although Moshi is working overtime on some new toys to pull apart the old buildings along the Bay Road."

"How is Moshi?"

"More forgetful than ever. I worry about him, gets worse every year."

Lindsey yawned loudly in her ear. Sabrina could hear the rustle of covers. "Do you have any cheery news or are you going to try to keep me awake with depressing things?"

"I checked the station records."

"Depressing things then. You trying to torture yourself?"

"The Orehem case is gone from the records. Wiped clean like he never existed," Sabrina said, flinging a rock down the hillside.

"The T-heads have it now. Even a civilian like me knows that."

"Of course they do. But there is a case at the hospital. Enough equipment for an entire O.R. was stolen from a loading dock. That should go to Sean and me. We're next in line for assignment. Instead, it's listed as unassigned."

"Didn't you say half of the cases never get solved anyway?" Lindsey said through another yawn.

"Yeah, but who can really find out who stole Ms. Randisharn's handbag? Who cares? She probably just forgot it somewhere. But the hospital—that is a crime that affects hundreds of people."

"Was anyone hurt in the attempt?"

"One security guard. He's still in a coma. If he doesn't wake up, a murder charge will be added. Then it might get some attention."

"Here is hoping for murder then," Lindsey chirped.

Sabrina laughed. "No, I hope he is fine. I might put my uncle in a coma if this keeps up, though."

"All the more reason to go to Lysander for school."

"I'm sure you will get to Lysander Arts, but my grades stink. Every time I try to study, I just think I would rather be outside running."

"Can you read on duty there?"

"Then I'd really fall asleep. I'm not allowed. Not even allowed to talk to you."

"I'm calling the police."

Sabrina's laugher was cut short by a red flash in her vision. "I got to go. The sensors are picking something up below. Probably just a deer, but I need to investigate."

"Go to it. I'm going back to sleep."

Sabrina flipped to a map of the hill. Green dots represented the other cadets. They were clustered in twos, something they often did at this time of night. One slept under a tree or in a strand of bushes while another kept lookout, less for scrits than for supervisors who might be dropping in for a surprise visit.

She was alone, her dot isolated by wide gaps of blackness. She heard a mechanical whine from higher up the hill: an all-terrain robot with built in flood lights and additional weaponry. It tracked her motions as she moved—the only partner willing to work with her. A second sensor flashed on her screen. Something below was coming toward her. She decided to radio in her position to the other cadets.

"Noted," an apathetic voice replied without identifying himself or offering any backup. None of the dots on the far side of the mountain budged.

"Is it because I am a woman?" she had once asked Sean.

Her yearning for his company manifested as a pang in her chest as she ducked beneath the branches of a fig tree.

"Half right," he had said. "Cause you are a woman who is a better shot, a better fighter, and a better officer than all them."

She smiled at the memory and moved with greater determination toward her target. A third sensor tripped, this one much closer. She dialed the all-terrain's controls to stop and deactivated its lights. She was in a thicket of tamarisk trees, their low hanging branches obscuring her vision. She moved her fingers to activate the infrared spectrum on her visor, fully expecting to see the outline of a deer, but as soon as she did, she was blinded by a flood of yellow while alarms screamed in her ears.

She snapped up the visor. Lights positioned in the trees had activated, bringing daylight to the patch of hillside. The green hues of the trees reappeared, branches whipped and snapped as a figure rushed out of the thicket and up the hill. His hair was a bush, his sandals worn so much that his cracked heels poked through the soles. His clothes were ripped and ragged, flapping as he ran. Beneath the rags, visible through the gaps and the tears, glistened skin that was shadowed with the distinct markings of a scrit.

He had been startled like a wild animal by the lights. Exposed now and entering the open, he made a straight path for the hilltop.

Sabrina slapped the call button on her communicator, "Cadet Sabryia, reporting a perimeter breach."

The words would automatically send her position to the other cadets. The all-terrain responded and spun its wheels to intercept the intruder. Her legs burned as she followed him up the slope. She was close enough to clearly see the writing that covered his body. Flowing script was tattooed over every inch from his neckline to his toes. She could even see the writing on his hands as he reached down in a graceful, balanced motion, picked up a large stick, and swung it at the approaching all-terrain.

Its light and camera shattered. The mechanical arm that had been probing outward to stun him went wide. A chorus of distress alarms sounded from the machine as it wheeled wildly, skidded in the loose gravel, then tumbled end-over-end down the hill.

So much for my partner.

A second bank of lights activated and poured light down on the barren stretch of open space between the intruder and the last fence. The foundation of the temple waited in the shadows beyond, wind tossing the heads of the weeds and grasses that grew from the cracks in the stone. Sabrina drew the stun rifle off her back and took aim.

"Stop or I will shoot."

Scrits were to be apprehended but never harmed, direct orders from her uncle himself. The intruder did not respond or slacken his pace. She charged the rifle, placed the crosshairs on him, and fired. The cylinder came spinning out with a buzz as its rear blades whirred through the air to stabilize. It struck the scrit in the torso, latching on to his clothes with mandibles. Immediately a blue arc of electric energy crackled in the air and dissipated.

Sabrina swore. His clothes were hanging so loosely that the cylinder had fired its charge from too far away. Now she was left looking at cloud of dust as he moved out of range of the rifle. He was above her, and that would not look good on a report. She sprinted after him as he approached another light that activated. She fired two more shots. One missed and the other discharged from a flap of his trousers. Some of the charge slowed him, causing him to limp as the muscles in his legs seized, but he showed astonishing strength and pushed onward.

A third bank of lights activated. Sabrina threw the rifle aside and drew a weighted snare from her belt. When she was close enough, she spun it in a circle past her ear three times, then released. The snare caught him in mid-stride, and he slammed into the ground with a gasp, the air knocked from his lungs. He was just a boy, a few years younger than Sabrina, his face youthful, not unlike many of her friends from school. He had a strong jaw with a glinting of gold whiskers running along it. His eyes were a mesmerizing blue, like the sky on a cloudless day. For an instant, he dug at the dirt like a dog looking for bones but then came to his senses, looking again at the fence ahead and back at Sabrina. She had her blaster out, set on stun. He reached to his belt and began to saw at the bindings on his leg with a knife.

"Drop the knife."

It was too late. He had already cut the bindings and leapt upwards in a swirl of clothes and muscle. The fighter in her had already assessed his strength and agility. He was strong, fast, and coordinated, but like most scrits, he was rash and dumb. More animal than human. Nonetheless, he would be dangerous to try and subdue by hand.

"Drop the knife or I'll shoot."

His feet were set in a wide stance. His eyes darted back and forth between her and his objective at the peak of the hill. The knife hovered in the air between them. She could read his intent as easily as she could an opponent in the ring. She fired.

He convulsed and fell backwards, but he rolled to his feet again and limped for the fence. A second stun after two partial shocks from the rifle might be too much for his system. All she needed now was a dead scrit on her record. She jogged after him. The knife was still in his right hand while his left covered the place where she had shot him. He was no longer even running. Instead he drew himself forward on one leg, dragging the other behind him. She approached him from an angle just as the last bank of lights activated, and she swept his legs out from beneath him with her foot. He dropped and rolled onto his back, still brandishing the knife. Her nostrils filled with the scent of his sweat and the musty smell of the desert that all scrits carried on them. She let him stagger to his feet again. Blood trickled from his forehead. His expression was dazed, his eyes beginning to water. His breath was ragged as he gasped through his lips, one of which was split and bleeding. Sabrina knew she could likely disarm him, but it was too late. He was fleeing again, his flight reduced to a pathetic limping walk, and finally a crawl. She pulled her microphone down close to her mouth.

"Charge the fence."

She knew officers kept score between cadets and scrits. A scrit netted before the last fence was a point for a cadet. If they reached the fence, it was a point for the scrits. Her class had had a perfect score, until now.

The scrit stumbled the last few steps, still clutching his abdomen. He would be sore there for days. He leapt onto the fence. The mesh was already charged, and he shuddered as he came into contact with it. It was a lower charge than a stun from her blaster and therefore safer.

Sabrina walked up behind him, waiting for the initial tremors to subside. His limbs sending up clouds of dust as spasms wracked his body. He was still clutching the knife, but it was not hard to pin his arm behind his back, lock his elbow, and force his grip to relax. The knife fell.

He swung at her with his free hand. It was comical and wide but angered something inside of her. She let her reflexes take control before she could think better of it, pivoting on her foot and using his momentum to swing him back into the fence. The charge was gone now, but the impact still took him unawares. His arm was firmly in her grasp. He did not realize yet that this fight was over, that he was a puppet on her string. He kicked at her. This resistance angered her even more, and the rhythm of combat took over. She delivered a punch to his lower back. Before his cry of pain ended, she turned on the ball of her foot and let fly a kick into the back of his knee. He dropped.

His eyes skittered from one side to the other. His resistance was gone. She punched him anyway, taking pleasure in the way her fist landed squarely on his cheek. She punched him again on his opposite temple and then in the center of his face, snapping his head backwards. When the other cadets appeared, he was coughing on blood pouring from his nose.

"He resisted," she said as one of her classmates neared. Five more brought up the rear, their weapons raised the carbon mesh and flex bands of their patrol suits glinting in the moonlight. Their visors were down over their eyes.

The quiet dark of the night was ruptured by a jet that sounded like a child's scream. The gravel underfoot, the electric fences, the other cadets, and the scrit were all cast in an eerie pale glow as an L'ved's dark bulk rose from a crest in the hill. The twin blue cones of flame from its turbines roared and crackled as the nozzles redirected the thrust. Tamarisk trees that had been waving gently in the breeze going out to sea, whipped and shook violently, leaves exploding outward as the machine passed over. Sabrina had not known it had been lurking so close. By the looks on the other cadet's faces, neither had they—the gold-ringed black dot that usually identified the machines on their survey maps had failed to appear. The L'ved passed overhead throwing up a backwash of dust and dried needles from the trees and filling the air with the acrid smell of methaline. Sabrina was careful not to be too distracted and kept a hand on the shoulder of her scrit. He had begun to tremble violently, his skin covered in a cold sweat. The other cadets strained their necks to watch the machine overhead, the reflection of the lights on its shoulders and chest sliding across their visors. Sabrina noticed the machine's head swivel, taking in the entire scene. Did it linger on her and the scrit? She could not tell before the machine banked and disappeared behind the shoulder of the ridge.

Cricket chirps returned. The gentle night breeze whispered in the trees. Sabrina could hear surf crashing down at the bottom of the hill. The cadets fell back into their roles, each demonstrating a sudden, earnest adherence to protocol, as if an instructor had appeared unexpectedly on the scene. Sabrina could not help rolling her eyes. She turned the scrit over, slapped bindings on his wrists and jerked him upright. The cadets stepped aside as she led him past. Unsteady and dazed, he nearly fell, Sabrina catching him by his salt-encrusted robe.

One of the other cadets slipped and fell on some of the scree underfoot trying to make way for them.

"All clear," she said, stepping past without offering a hand.

ἀ

Cruisers were parked in a valley between Hills 36 and 34. Sabrina pushed her prisoner into the back of one and set off for the station. The scrit had recovered and was keening, throwing his shoulders up against the sides of the vehicle. She glared at the switch that would seal the rear of the cruiser and infuse it with a gas that would sedate him. She did not trust the seals. Other officers complained of feeling groggy for hours after gassing prisoners.

"Quit it!" she yelled, punching the mesh grill, shaking it loudly in its fasteners. Her violence stunned him. He stopped, his face lost in the shadows, his head down. Sabrina breathed a sigh of relief and turned her eyes forward to the road when the message screen on the dash blinked. `Can mercy be found in the heart of she who was born of the stone, she the origin and the devourist of all things, she the mother without mercy?`

Sabrina slowed the cruiser and pulled off to the side of the road. She stared at the readout. The words remained, unblinking. With the cruiser stopped, she could hear the screech of an owl, the hiss of the surf just over the guard rail. Did she also hear the faint whine of an L'ved? If so the machine was distant and pulling away. She imagined moonlight glinting silver on its wings. The sky overhead was clear, full of stars. She turned back to the dashboard message screen.

Coastal Highway.NNW. Post 8. 23 minutes to HQ.

She rubbed her eyes.

What did I just see?

"Will you help me?"

The scrit had pressed his face to the mesh between the front seat and back. In the soft amber glow of the street lights, he was handsome. She thought it a shame that his mind was so ruined. She checked the dashboard message once more. It no longer seemed to be malfunctioning. With a check of her mirrors, she moved the cruiser back on to the road. On impulse she asked, "What is your name?"

"Seeker."

This is new, Sabrina thought.

"Where are you from, Seeker?" she said, discretely flicking on the voice recorder.

"I … I … I am not supposed to tell you."

"No, it's all right. I'm here to help you."

"You are one of the Nazreen. We … I am not to speak to you," he said, turning over his hands. "I am here to seek."

"Seek what?"

He said nothing. They drove on for a little longer, and she noticed him looking alarmed. Already his memory had reset. Like all scrits, he could not retain more than a few minutes of memories.

"Where am I?"

"You are safe, I'm here to help you," she said. "What is your name?"

He looked around the backseat, as if noticing it for the first time. He grimaced and his eyes alighted on his hands. Sabrina noticed him studying them, reading them.

"I am Seeker."

"Where are you from, Seeker?"

"I'm not supposed to tell you."

Sabrina sighed and checked the time left before she reached headquarters. Less than 15 minutes. The young man grimaced and shook his hands, flexing and unflexing them.

"Do your hands hurt?"

He nodded. She pulled the car over to the side of the road again. On a hunch, she reached across the seat and opened the med kit. She shook a can of steri-spray, then opened a latch on the mesh barrier between them. He recoiled.

"Just put your hands through. I promise it will help." She sprayed her own hand first. Only then did he slowly squeeze through both bound hands. She sprayed. The shadows mixed seamlessly with the dark markings on his skin. His palms, where he had fallen, were cut in several places. When she was finished, he retracted his hands.

"Better?" she asked. He nodded. She turned back to the wheel.

"Please help me. I'm scared. I can't remember anything …." He reached up to touch his head and gasped when he found blood on his hands.

She knew her foot should simply press the accelerator, but instead she watched as a hand—her hand—turned off the voice recorder. For a moment they both sat in silence. She tried to focus her mind on a question to ask him, but those gibberish words from the dashboard were seared in her mind. *Can mercy be found in the heart of she who was born of the stone ...*

She could feel his eyes on her while she stared out the windscreen. A civilian roll pod passed going in the opposite direction, its headlights sending a spiny mouse on the shoulder capering into the bushes.

"I'm Sabrina. What is your name?"

"Jacob."

Her heart began to beat in her ears. She fought the urge to turn the recorder back on, afraid he would notice and stop cooperating.

"Where are you from, Jacob?" She turned slowly in her seat.

He seemed to think hard, as if trying to recall a faded memory. "The desert."

"Where in the desert?"

"I can't remember."

"Don't look down. Look at me. When you think of the desert, whom do you see?"

"A woman. My mother. She fled there, with the others."

"What others?"

"Others who were fleeing."

"What were they fleeing from? Was it war?"

"Something like that, but something worse ... I can't remember." He rocked forward and struck his head with the heels of his hand.

"No, Jacob, you are doing so well. Who else was in the desert?" she said. She wanted to put a hand on his shoulder to sooth his agitation, but the best she could do was place her hand against the screen between them. His eyes focused on it a moment, he tilted his hand to the side and his expression changed, as if he was looking on another scene playing before him.

"There were people there already. They were once our enemies but we … what is on my hands?"

"Just some ink, Jacob. It will come off. Tell me about those people who were your enemies."

"They were darker. I was afraid of them, but they helped us."

"Why are they out in the desert?"

"To be safe from the rays."

"The sun's rays? The desert does not seem to be a good place to avoid the sun's rays."

"No. No, something worse. Something in the city." He flexed his wrists against his bindings, the muscles in his arms rock hard, his foot kicking the screen, "I can't remember."

"You are doing great, Jacob. What was in the city?"

"I can't remember. What … what am I doing here?" He began to look back and forth, pressing his hands against the windows.

"Jacob, tell me more about what you remember about the desert. How do you survive?"

"In caves near springs. And the watchers … they watch over us."

"Who are the watchers?"

"The ones from above. Sometimes they come down. I remember when there was a sickness they came down to heal us, but others … others threw rocks at them. Especially the old."

He was making no sense to her any longer. She decided to change her line of questioning.

"Jacob, why did you come here?"

"Because God is here."

The interior of the cruiser felt like it was suddenly shrinking from the weight of the night outside. Sabrina felt a shiver travel up from deep inside her gut to her shoulders, neck, even scalp. "Don't say that word, Jacob. Don't *ever* say that word."

His breaths came rapidly and he threw himself to the far side of the seat, away from her.

"You are one of them. Oh no, no! Let me go!" He began to flail and kick at the sides of the cruiser. The vehicle rocked back and forth with his motions. Sabrina started the cruiser again. Eventually he exhausted himself, then seemed to forget why he was panicked. He looked around as if waking up.

"Where am I?"

Sabrina checked the navigation screen. Eight minutes to the station.

"I'm here to help," she said but could not conceal the exasperation in her voice this fourth time around. He was reading his hands again.

"Jacob," she said. He looked up for a moment at the sound of the name. A smile crossed his lips, then faded and was replaced by a scowl. "What is on the mountain?"

"My name is Seeker."

Chapter 8
Durp and Xandes

Jacob winced when the harsh light of the station detention zone shined through the cruiser windows. He had tried to remember more for her during the drive, but his efforts had been futile, his attempts ending with him pounding his head with the heels of his tattooed hands.

"I just don't have the words," he said. As she pulled to a stop, he turned his face downward into his clasped hands and mumbled fervently, praying.

Two detention officers, dressed in white, their bodies padded with rubber armor, waited outside the vehicle, each clutching a sedation stick. Sabrina winced with the memory of being charged with one—all cadets were required to experience what it felt like to be on the receiving end. It was far from a sedate experience. Half the class had lost control of their bowels, more than half their bladders.

As she got out and the officers moved to the back of the cruiser, Sabrina felt a surge of protectiveness.

"Wait, this one is calm," she said. "At least for me."

She did not like the looks they gave her. The shorter one was named Rai. The pores of his flat nose stood out, black with dirt. He was a friend of Pitt and Boyle. The taller one was classmate of hers named Andrew. Both lowered their sticks in Jacob's direction. Sabrina grimaced and lifted the door open. Jacob was trembling when she pulled him out. The bright lights of the bay cast him in a sickly pallor. There was more blood on him than she had realized. She had lost control, and she knew it. A wave of guilt rolled over her and she rubbed her neck.

"Looks like you already subdued him pretty well," Rai laughed. Andrew looked back and forth between them before joining in the laughter.

Jacob moved closer to her. He was trembling.

"*Heyzoo,* this one seems absolutely besotted with you," Rai said. "Maybe we should have more lady officers after all."

"Shut it," she said. But he was right. Jacob was cowering against her, staring up at her imploringly. Didn't he remember her beating him?

"He put up a good fight. Had a knife on him," she said shoving him towards the door. "You both coming, or you going to stand around with your sticks up your asses?"

They followed, but neither held his stick at the ready. When they reached the processing desk, Rai and Andrew peeled off and entered the back office where Sabrina could hear a game of pitchball on the wall screen. At this hour, it must have been a recording, but it still interested the guards more than processing a prisoner.

Xandes, an administrative officer who had graduated two years before Sabrina, waited at the desk. She had a pinched face and dark circles under her eyes, circles that stood out all the more against her pale skin. Her blond hair was pulled into a tight ponytail. Sabrina had suspected that she had wanted to be a street officer, but like most female cadets, had been forced into a desk position. Xandes' eyes passed over Sabrina's patrol suit, and she was nearly successful in suppressing a frown before she took down a palm screen and began typing.

"Location?"

"Hill 36. Southeast face."

"Elevation?"

There was no reason for her to ask except that she, too, was keeping score.

"Area 11."

Her eyebrows lifted but her eyes did not move from the screen. Sabrina decided not to volunteer the information that Jacob actually reached the fence. Xandes would hear soon enough.

"Has he been interrogated?"

"Yes. He said …" Sabrina stopped, shamed by a strange sense of confidence, "Mostly gibberish. I captured some on the voice recorder."

"Always is," Xandes said, checking off a box on the screen.

"His hands were burning though. I found the steri-spray helped."

"Uhh huh. Press his thumb here," Xandes said, holding out the palm screen. Sabrina helped Jacob reach over the counter and touch the screen. When the screen beeped, Xandes spoke into the comm-piece on her collar. "Processing call."

A moment later, Alex Durp stepped out of the office where the two detention guards had disappeared. The sounds of the game drifted out from the open door.

"Well, if it isn't Princess Cadet."

Sabrina stiffened. "Officer Durp, a little late for you to do intake," she said.

Durp scratched the expansive lump of flesh that hung over his belt. He had not shaved in days, and crumbs lingered in his whiskers. His shirt was dark with grease stains. Sabrina and others considered him a disgrace to the uniform, but he had close friends in influential places— like Pitt and Boyle—and he ran a tight detention block. There had never been an escape on his watch. His gut was misleading. Although he was overweight, his shoulder muscles still strained against the largest of shirts, and his arms were as thick as most men's thighs. It was said that when walking the detention block, he did not even bother with armor or a sedation stick.

"Thomas was sick, so I'm filling in for him."

"I heard something is going around. That is charitable of you, sir."

He gave out a false chuckle. Xandes stood between them, staring at the floor, her hands balled into fists.

"The boys tell me that this one was besotted with you," he said, looking over at Jacob and shifting his weight from one foot to the other. "I just wanted to come out and see it for myself."

Sabrina tried hard not to look at Jacob, but she felt him trembling.

"He's no different than any other prisoner, sir."

"Is that right? Well, having both your princesses might tame all these wretches. Maybe there is a use for female officers after all." He let out another chuckle and headed back to his office.

"Officer Durp, aren't you going to process the prisoner?" Xandes said to his back.

"You can do it, Xandes. We're watching the game."

"Sir?" Xandes said, her inflection rising, but he had already shut the door. She slammed down the palm screen and yanked an oversized sedation stick from a locker. It whined as she charged it. She rounded the counter and yanked Jacob away by the collar.

"Sabrina!" Jacob cried.

Xandes stopped. Jacob was holding the edge of the counter, staring at Sabrina. Xandes looked back and forth between them, as if not believing what she was witnessing. Sabrina did not know how to respond. In the silence of her hesitation, Jacob spoke again. "Sabrina, please don't leave me."

Xandes grinned, revealing small teeth that were so white they were almost translucent, "*Heyzoo,* they were right. He is besotted with you. How did he learn your name? How did he *remember* it?"

"Must have caught it from one of the other officers."

"Then why isn't he calling you Cadet Sabryia?"

"I don't know," Sabrina said. "But if it makes it easier, I'll come along—to help you process him."

Xandes seemed to weigh the option in her mind before nodding and motioning for Sabrina to follow. She shoved Jacob ahead of her and leveled the end of the stick at him, its prongs hovering just behind his bowed neck. They passed by the door to the office as a point was scored in the pitchball match. The men's furious cheers spilled out into the hall.

"Daldo! Daldo! Daldo!" they chanted the name of their favorite player.

"Where are you taking me?" Jacob asked.

"Shut up," Xandes said.

"Just a room where you can rest for the night," Sabrina said, although it earned her a scowl from Xandes.

"First, we're going to wash the stink off you," Xandes said, turning Jacob around a corner and guiding him into a dark room. A rubber mat covered the floor, and the air smelled damp. Xandes pushed Jacob to the center of the room, removed his bindings, and ordered him to take off his clothes. Sabrina remained in the doorway, noting the camera ports in the corners of the room and wondering if anyone was watching or if the pitchball match was being broadcast on all internal monitors.

He removed his shirt, revealing a chiseled frame overlaid with extravagant tattoos. There was a slight smile at the corner of Xande's mouth. She flicked the switch of the stick on and off, allowing a small spark to arc between prongs. "All of them," she added.

Jacob slipped off his straw sandals. They were so worn that, once removed, they surrendered any resemblance to shoes. Still, Jacob placed them neatly side by side on the mat next to his folded shirt. He turned aside, removed his trousers, balled them in his hands and covered his crotch with them.

Xandes crossed to the corner where a hose was hung, taking it in her free hand and aiming the nozzle at Jacob. "Drop the trousers," she said, punctuating the sentence with a warning shot of spray in his face.

Jacob turned Sabrina's way, but she could not meet his eye. He looked pathetic, smeared in dirt, blood, his hair askew. His pulse was racing in his neck. He set his trousers beside his shirt. Xandes made no effort to be discreet as her eyes studied Jacob's nakedness. Her lips puckered, and she sent a sidelong glance at Sabrina before squeezing the nozzle and sending a jet of water into Jacob's crotch, doubling him over. He turned his back to her to protect himself while Xandes' laughter echoed in the chamber.

"He looks nice from this side, too," Xandes said, shaking the hose.

"Xandes, are you here to wash him or torture him?" Sabrina said.

VOLUME I – THE CITY

Xandes shrugged and turned the blast of water on Jacob's head. Some inevitably went into his eyes, nose, and mouth, and he began to cough. Xandes giggled at this. He raised a hand as if to block the water. After a glare from Sabrina, Xandes sighed loudly and removed the stream from his face. While Jacob recovered, blinking the water out of his eyes, she nonchalantly turned it on his sandals. They seemed to dissolve as the stream of water swept them out of his reach. They swirled about the drain before all but the largest pieces were sucked away.

Xandes twisted the nozzle head, and the stream became more of a mist. She ordered Jacob to stand up, his arms held out at his sides. The grit and blood washed away. Water foamed and cascaded off his muscular stomach. As she stared at his body, Sabrina did feel a certain tug deep inside her. It was not carnal. Standing in the cold water, his sex was shrunken and did not draw Sabrina's gaze the way it did Xandes'. Instead, she was mesmerized by the writing, the script flowing over his body. In his nakedness, it was revealed in its completeness. It was beautiful. Proportionate, balanced, like a complete thought captured. Sabrina was seized with the same feeling she had when studying one of Lindsey's paintings, as if she were looking at something of ineffable beauty, beyond her ability to produce or describe. The writing had the grace of flickering flames and, once revealed, Jacob seemed to draw strength from it. He stood straighter; his chin up, his eyes closed in serenity.

As if to challenge his rediscovered dignity, Xandes narrowed the stream again and made Jacob turn while she sprayed it into his backside. Sabrina crossed her arms to convey her impatience. Xandes finally turned off the water. From a locker in the corner, she removed a towel and threw it to him. While he dried himself, she produced a med kit, removing a jar of salve and bandages.

"You'll have to apply this." She smiled and tossed them to Sabrina. She caught the first aid items and stepped forward, telling Jacob to kneel and place his hands behind his back. He cooperated while she snapped a restraining seal around his wrists and then began to open the salve container. So close to him, she was aware of his eyes. Even within the dim lighting of the showers, they were an electric blue. He had been washed free of the desert, but it was still present between them in the dirt on her uniform, drifting off to form a muddy swirl on the floor.

She cleaned and dressed the gash on his forehead, then turned to one on his shoulder. As she covered it with a bandage, she felt remorse at concealing the flowing script.

"The writing, it's beautiful. Why do you all have it?"

"So we don't forget."

"Don't forget what?"

"To seek the temple and to return."

"Return where?"

"The desert." He stared down at the dust from her boots mixing with the water and slipping away toward the drain. Then his eyes focused on her with an urgent intensity. "Sabrina, you will go there. I know you will. It's where you will find the truth."

Sabrina's hand froze where she touched his skin.

"What are you two lovers saying?" Xandes asked from across the room. It startled Jacob. His thoughts seemed to scatter like autumn leaves in a wind and confusion returned to his face. "Where am I?"

"Nice job interrupting an interrogation," Sabrina spat over her shoulder.

"If that is what you want to call it," Xandes said, throwing a white gown their way. It fell on the floor. Sabrina tried to pick it up quickly from the wet shower floor, but it was damp as she slid it over Jacob. It looked ugly and awkward on his frame, especially with the script now partially covered. The points, glyphs, and serifs peeked out as if struggling to free themselves.

The two women led him down a corridor to a heavy door with a thick glass window. Xandes typed a code into the keypad next to it.

Sabrina took a long breath before it opened. "Don't be scared," she said to Jacob. "You can rest here tonight. You will be safe."

The door slid to the side. Lights flicked on the moment Xandes entered, revealing a hall the length of a pitchball field. Identical doors with hexagonal windows faced each other from either side. Xandes marched past them, her eyes fixed ahead of her, the muscles in her jaws working. As soon as she passed by the first door, the screaming began. Hands, covered in the same black writing as Jacob's, pounded at the glass. Sabrina tightened her grip on Jacob. His eyes were wide with terror. Panicked voices called out.

"Help! Please! Where am I?"

"Please, let me out! What did I do?"

Sabrina could not imagine the confusion and utter horror of waking in a place and not knowing how she had arrived there. To make this discovery multiple times, as her memory reset over and over again, as it would for a scrit, made her stomach twist and ache.

Xandes must have read the concern in her face. In an odd moment of understanding she said, "They won't remember this place once they are rehabilitated. It's unpleasant, but necessary, so they won't hurt themselves."

Sabrina nodded. She knew all scrits would be sent, eventually, to a rehabilitation center. Her uncle had assured her that there were treatments for scrits and that they could make a recovery that allowed them to live happily the rest of their lives. But where they came from in the first place, what the occultists had done to them, she was not sure. No one was. Her uncle had only said that they were a tragedy that required patience, mercy, and understanding. Sabrina had never met a recovered scrit, but it was not an experience she would openly share if she had been rehabilitated. Maybe she knew rehabilitated scrits and did not even realize it.

She wondered if Jacob had a family he had run away from. Had he fallen into the clutches of occultists who had brainwashed him? Would he be able to return to his family? Were they looking for him? She had processed dozens of scrits and, until this night, had never cared. They were mainly a nuisance. But now one had told her his name. He had become a person.

She noticed a gloved hand thumping at a window. She had heard that while they waited to be shipped out, some scrits became truly deranged, scratching at the walls of the cells until their nails peeled away from their fingers. These had to be protected from themselves. First the gloves. Then came gags to keep them from using their teeth to chew at the gloves. Some were placed in padded cells.

Animals.

"When is the next transport?" Sabrina asked.

"There is one tomorrow morning," Xandes said. "That's why so many of the cells are full."

She keyed open one of the last doors. A faint whiff of urine drifted out. Jacob slowed, starting to resist. Sabrina stiffened her own grip on him. Xandes stepped inside to inspect the room. It was empty but for a toilet and a sleeping pallet against the wall.

"What is going to happen to me?" Jacob asked, holding his ground outside the door. Out of the corner of her eye, Sabrina noticed Xandes lowering the sedation stick.

"You will spend the night here," Sabrina said, putting some steel into her voice. "In the morning they will take you somewhere to restore your memories."

"But wait— ..."

"Trust me," Sabrina said, willing herself to detach from the whole situation, aware that she had lost the distance that professionalism required. Where was Sean when she needed him? "You will be fine, Jacob. I promise."

He looked to Xandes, who had her thumb poised to depress the charge on the sedation stick. He relented and let Sabrina lead him into the room, where she sat him down on the sleeping pallet. She turned immediately to leave, avoiding the imploring expression on his face and his eyes full of hope and terror. The door slid shut behind her and Xandes. She walked swiftly away while Xandes typed in a code to secure the cell, after which she tried to catch up with Sabrina.

"Jacob?" Xandes asked, her eye brow cocked as she came alongside Sabrina. "You did not mention that he shared his name with you."

"Must have slipped my mind," Sabrina said, busying herself with her belt. "Can't even be sure that's really his name." Her visor, hooked onto her hip, was vibrating. She grabbed it, but knew she could not answer it in the hall, as the chorus of pounding and pleading had begun anew.

"Shut it!" Xandes screamed, rapping on the windows with the stick. Her voice rose with every door she passed. "Shut it. Shut it. *Shut it.*"

Sabrina reached the end of the corridor and was grateful to have the door closed between her and Xandes, silencing the sound of the detention officer's voice. She opened her visor. It was Sean. Relief coursed through her. She snapped it onto her forehead and noticed the hour. It was morning.

"I got a lead on our friend with the knife," Sean said.

Sabrina wondered how he even knew about Jacob as she had not yet filed a report, but then she realized he meant Orehem.

"The one who tried to add some ventilation to your armpit?"

"The very. The deed for the shop was co-signed by an Anselem Jackson. I've got his address in my hand. I say we do some surveillance."

"Are you back?" She asked, listening to the background noise of conversations, footsteps, and intercoms that sounded like the station office.

"Discharged yesterday."

She leaned against the wall, the muscles in her back relaxing. She caught sight of her face in the screen of a blank detention monitor. She was grinning like a school girl. Sean described how he got an early discharge from the hospital. She half-listened. If he was calling her, she deduced that D'Ag's order for her to be assigned to scrit duty had yet to filter down to Sean. Her uncle assumed that she would follow his orders without question. She had not slept all night. Sean was just beginning his shift and probably wondering why she was late.

"I'll be there in ten minutes."

Chapter 9

Anselem Jackson

Daldo stared at Sabrina from the mural on the wall of a house on the end of a row. He was wearing his green and white Roosen team jersey, his number 0 emblazoned on his chest and emanating light nearly as bright as the glow from behind his head. His facial features were stylized and idealized, his cheekbones sharper, his lips fuller, his eyes were irritatingly half-closed, as if he was drowsy. Off to the side in miniature were depictions of him in various moves: diving to catch a pitchball, tackling another player, tumbling in the air like an acrobat. If she squinted, the depictions of his lithe body and those of his opponents resembled birds hovering about his head.

"I should take that woman in for that … monstrosity," Sabrina said when the owner of the house, a roundish woman in a gray dress, dragged a rusty cart of groceries to the stoop and began to fumble with her keys.

"You don't even know if she painted it," Sean said from the seat beside her. "Likely she had nothing to do with it. Just woke up one morning, and there it was, painted by hooligans."

"You'd mind more if it was a Jenis club player up there," she said.

"I would, but only because the lot of them are so ugly."

They were in a worn-out CRP with cloudy windows, faded paneling and instruments with their buttons worn smooth. The seats had lost their stuffing long ago. Both of them were dressed in civilian clothes, Sean in a blue pullover and brown trousers, one of the new cuts available that year. Sabrina wore an orange blouse and green trousers over her patrol suit. Their clothes were loose in order to conceal their weapons.

Sean leaned over from the driver's seat and took a closer look at the side of the house.

"No candles, stones, flags, or even a basin. It does not qualify as a point of worship. It's technically just art." He was baiting her. It was mid-afternoon. They had been trailing their mark, Anselem Jackson, all day, following him on a trip to the clothing store where he was a procurement manager and on a few visits to his distributors. Anselem had grabbed lunch from a vendor on the street before returning to his office, where he had been working at his desk since.

Despite the initial thrill of tracking a possible lead, not to mention the thought of going against her uncle's wishes, Sabrina was drowsy. After a lunch of brick-oven bread slathered in olive spread and rosemary, she suspected she was not the only one. Sean's head had nodded towards the steering wheel a few times. She cradled a cup of tea between her legs, but the relaxing warmth on her thighs was having the opposite effect than she intended. Banter was what they needed.

She considered Sean's suggestion that the horribly proportioned and clearly illegal depiction of Daldo was art. She decided it was not. Art was what Lindsey created. This eyesore before her was just obscene.

"I bet if you checked the ground underneath you'd find candle droppings. The work is clearly deifying him."

"After that goal he scored in the match against Trilander …"

"Not you, too."

Sean smiled and readjusted himself. It took him some time to find a comfortable position in the old, worn-out seats. A spring had been digging into Sabrina's thigh all morning.

"He's just a guy, Cadet. In a couple years, his numbers will drop and there will be some other guy."

She remembered one of her uncle's comments about being in the center of a cheering multitude and how it could affect the psyche. Sean broke into her thoughts.

"Come on, some of my favorite memories are of playing on the pitch and watching games with my friends. There is no harm in having pitchball heroes."

It was hard for Sabrina to argue the point. She loved to play. Keep the ball from opposing players, pass it to your own, or put it in the net. It was an artificial world, free of the complexities of real life, of relationships, of sexism, of injustice. It was the fairest field she knew besides the boxing ring. If all that mattered was physical ability, she could always excel.

"People get around the flag thing," she said. "At a game the other day, I saw people waving red-and-blue dish towels when Trilander scored."

"I imagine the old man will speak to the minister of dish towels, and those colors will be discontinued next year."

"There is no minister of dish towels," she said, although she would not put it past her uncle to speak to the minister of manufacturing and commerce to ensure that such colors were discontinued. "I've heard it said that sports are just ritualized violence, a release valve for our violent natures."

Sean's eyes seemed to lose focus for a moment as he stared straight ahead. In one hand he held his cooling tea, with the other he picked at the cracked steering wheel. "You know Sabrina, sometimes I wonder … all this the Head Ministry does, all this we do, to keep religion in check, to keep the sects from returning and wreaking havoc on our copasetic existence here. I wonder if it's all misplaced. Is religion the source of all evil, or is it us?"

He turned to look at her, and she felt empty. She had not expected the conversation to go in this direction. After her long, unresponsive silence, he continued, "Even the sports, we talk about them so much up here in Fortinbras. Up in Lysander, it's all about fashion."

"That is where the clothing manufacturers are."

"But why did the Founders place them there? It does sometimes seem like a big experiment. One city focused on sports, the other on fashion."

As if on cue, a group of schoolchildren crossed the street in front of the CRP, then turned up the sidewalk. Half wore red shirts pulled over their uniforms, half blue shirts. One of D'Ag's experimental schools. To Sabrina's dismay, she could not help but notice how the children wearing the same colors clumped together.

"Maybe the experiments are needed," she said.

Sean sipped his tea. "I don't want to be a test rat. Science has been used for some pretty evil things, too."

Sabrina drank from her own cup, chewed her lip, then offered a new subject. "I saw Officer Dentry this morning. His arm was in a cast. Do you know what happened?"

"Yeah," Sean said with a chuckle. "Got too close to an L'ved."

"Are you serious?"

He nodded, his eyes again scanning the street. "Came across a nest of occultists. Called in for reinforcements. An L'ved was nearby, swung in low. The occultists panicked. Tried fighting it." He shook his head. "Stupid. The old wasps are not lethal … at least they are programmed not to be. They'll shock and stun before they will kill."

Not unlike our orders for the capture of scrits, Sabrina thought.

"But then how did Dentry get hurt?"

"The occultists crossed the line. I don't know what happens or what does it, but once those things decide to take you out, you're dead. They are supposed to be able to recognize an officer by the suit, but well, nothing is perfect. Dentry is lucky to be alive."

Sabrina gripped her cup more tightly. She wondered if D'Ag was aware of the force the L'veds were using.

"Have you ever seen them kill?"

Sean shook his head. "No, but I saw the aftermath. I was a cadet. There was a den of occultists, and we called in the T-heads who called in an L'ved. I saw the room where the L'ved cornered those people." His eyes glazed over again. "I don't eat meat any more after that. Can't stand the smell."

"What makes them switch over to being lethal?"

He shook his head and pressed his lips into a thin line. "I don't know. Whatever they feel like."

"They are machines. They don't *feel*. It must be a programming protocol."

Sean shrugged and sipped his tea. "Think what you want. Those things, they don't move like machines."

"You think they are remotely controlled, by some T-man somewhere?"

"You mean from Third City?"

It was Sabrina's turned to shrug. Third City was a belief among most people within the walls. Children made rhymes about it and referred to it as "Turd City." It was where older siblings threatened to send younger siblings if they did not behave.

"Third City is a myth."

"Then where do the T-men live?"

Her uncle had explained to her that the special investigators had to keep their identities secret, but that they lived among the folk of Lysander and Fortinbras, just like anyone else. There was no "Third City." But she could not share that with Sean. When she had asked D'Ag if myths about imaginary cities among the populace disturbed him, he had laughed. "When they start talking about imaginary 'kingdoms,' I'll be worried, but not Third City."

"They probably have to keep their identities secret," she said carefully. "They probably live right next door, and we don't know it."

"I'll entertain that," Sean said. "But then where do the L'veds stay?"

"I don't know, D'Ag's bed chamber."

Sean laughed, almost spilling his tea. Sabrina smiled, but her mind was preoccupied with his question: where *did* they stay? She had never seen a nest of them within the Head Ministry, although she knew there were rooms where she was not allowed to go. For some reason, the image from her dream a few days before came to mind: the white marble walls, a single glass column, a silver sphere inside ….

"Where did they come from in the first place?" she asked.

"I always thought our dear leader created them. After all, they weren't around when our parents were kids."

Sabrina wondered, her hand touching her uniform sleeve. Pictures of Moshi's laboratory came to mind. *If not D'Ag ...*

All this talk of her uncle was making her uncomfortable. She did not want to reveal too much to Sean, but at the same time, she was becoming aware of so many mysteries she had never questioned.

"I always wondered why they had the street names changed," she found herself saying.

"Me, too!" Sean said. "When I was growing up in Lysander, we used to play a game where we would try to find old names on street corners, pavements, curbs, the sides of houses, anywhere that the censors had missed. We had a whole collection of old street signs, bits of broken letters, and charcoal rubbings we made of engraved letters that had not been sanded away."

"That was so illegal," Sabrina said breathlessly.

Sean shook his head at the memory, staring out through the windscreen. "I know. We'd all be rehabilitated for it now." He sat up with a jerk, the flattened springs in the seat groaning. "Game on, Cadet."

Anselem Jackson had stepped out of his office and onto the sidewalk. Sabrina set down her cup. Anselem walked off in the opposite direction. When she was certain he was not turning around, she opened the door of the CRP and followed.

Anselem was a tall man, a head above just about every other person he passed on the sidewalk. It made him easy to follow. As casually as possible, Sabrina, steered herself into the flow of foot traffic behind him. From what she had seen of his face, he was in need of a shave. His eyes rested in deep sockets below a gloomy, dark brow. His hair was tapered closely on the sides but was overlong in the back, resting on the collar of his jacket. The jacket itself was standard issue, but it was old, its cut having been declared "out of style" in Lysander at least five seasons ago. Sean had thought nothing of it, but Sabrina found a clothes merchant, wearing an out-of-style jacket suspicious.

Don't presume. She reminded herself. Justice required a disinterested mind.

Anselem's shoulders swayed, his head bowed. Like many tall men, he seemed uncomfortable with his height. He turned off the main boulevard and headed west towards the wharves. Street vendors rolled in and out of the quays, their carts full of fresh fish, while two noticeably old and out-of-shape officers scanned the fish for radiation. It was not one of the more prestigious duties for officers. Most often it was seen as punishment or last stop before retirement.

Lose Anselem, and it will be all I ever get to do.

She turned her face from the officers in case one recognized her. Anselem went north next. Sabrina took her bearings. They were moving towards the Blocks through a neighborhood that was a patchwork of reclaimed and non-reclaimed houses. New residences with shining fixtures and freshly painted shutters faced dusty buildings with boarded windows, their doors sealed with the crest of the Security Ministry, prohibiting entry. She had been on more than a few calls, arresting the occasional homeless man or curious adolescent in such shells of houses. Twice she had found scrits, one alive, one dead from dehydration. At first glance, there was nothing objectionable within the sealed houses she had been inside. They often looked eerily normal, just like any other house would while its residents were out: magazines had been left open on couches; antique communication devices rested in charging ports; a purse, a backpack hung beside a door. She had tripped over children's brightly colored toys more than a few times.

But the insidious did lurk. In almost every home there were grotesque signs left from the sects that had dominated life: scrolls containing superstitions rolled tightly into cylinders and nailed to the walls as talismans, suns displayed on candle sticks, swords of all materials, wood, metal, polished stone—some so grotesque as to have a figurine of a corpse stretched across them. These things shared walls with family photographs, calendars, thermostat controls—the mundane things of daily life so permeated with poison that no one even noticed. Insanity had become so common that it no longer seemed unusual. The victims of the Cataclysm had tumbled towards the abyss in complete ignorance. It was no surprise to her that the catastrophe had caught so many of these people unaware, only that anyone survived at all.

The pace of traffic, vehicle and foot, slowed on this street. Residents visited on front stairs while children played on the sidewalks. Anselem stood out with his quick pace and his lowered head, as if he had some important destination to reach and a schedule to keep. Everyone else moved leisurely, greeting and gossiping with their neighbors. Sabrina slowed and made small talk with a few women sitting on stairs while their children played in the street. When she looked up, she noticed Anselem disappearing into a house. It was a condemned building, but the plastic seal molded to the door had been split down its center. It was too dangerous to follow him inside, so she continued down the block past three more houses. When she was certain she was hidden by the angle of the windows, she ducked into the next alleyway.

The alley was overgrown with weeds that left a yellow residue on her trousers. An empty can crunched beneath her foot. The end of the alley was blocked with scraps of warped and rotting wood fallen from the ruins of an old factory. An exposed nail snagged her coat and ripped it with a loud tear. From the windows above her head, she heard two children singing, a wall screen playing, and a mother calling for one of her children. A teenage boy answered back in uninterested tones.

At the very back of the alley, another noise caught her attention: a door, scraping the ground as it opened. She peered slowly around the corner to see the door opening, the seal of the ministry peeling off its face. Anselem emerged into the tiny space behind the houses. He descended a set of rickety metal stairs in her direction. She spun back around before he could see her, listening carefully: his footsteps, his own trousers brushed by the copious weeds, the sounds of planks of wood being set aside, the rasp of what sounded like a metal gate opening. Then nothing.

She waited a few more beats, her hand dropping to the blaster at her waist before she turned the corner.

Anselem was gone. She snapped her blaster out of her holster. The windows of the factory shell were high up, higher than the houses' roofs. The wall was solid brick, unbroken by a door, but there was a stairwell leading down to a utility grate set below ground. The boards Anselem had positioned to the side were leaning up against the wall next to the stairs. The grate was large enough for him to have passed through.

She could not follow. The grate would make too much noise as she opened it. But she could not afford to lose him now. He was clearly up to something.

She decided to do away with her jacket, balling it up and tossing it into the weeds. Her trousers followed, revealing the rest of her patrol suit. A tingle ran up through her fingers as she pulled on the gloves, and they interfaced with her nervous system through derm links.

"Check in, Ace," Sean said when she pulled on her visor.

"He crossed through a council-sealed house into an abandoned factory of some sort. I lost him when he went in through a grate that is loud enough to be heard in Lysander. I am going to see if there is another way I can enter from the roof."

"The factory is council-sealed, too. I'm looking at its door on the other side. I'm parked by the subway entrance."

"We have him on any number of violations that we could take him in on."

"Keep following. He's doing more than taking a casual walk. Let's see where he's going."

"Affirmative."

The grips on her fingertips and boots activated and bit into the skin of the factory. The wall was an easy climb. She threw herself over the crest and onto a roof filled with weeds springing up through cracks in the tarred shingles. Moldy tarpaulins rolled in the breeze, secured by only a few remaining nails. A rusty metal door to a stairwell hung wide open on the far side of the roof. The vegetation muffled her steps, but the stairwell was not as kind, her weight alone made it creak, and it was covered with shards of glass from a shattered skylight. She reactivated the grips on her boots and gloves for extra traction and descended on the stairwell's support beams.

The air inside the factory was hot and close. The odor of the air was a mixture of mold and desiccated linoleum. No longer on the questionable staircase, Sabrina moved more quickly, pausing briefly at doorways and corners to listen. She heard nothing. Finally, the corridors of offices and storage areas opened to the wide expanse of the factory floor. A ray of afternoon sunlight ran from the line of windows down to crowded rows of idled machinery. Anselem was threading a path from one row to the next, his footsteps echoing loudly. Sabrina threw herself into a crouch and moved forward until the cement floor beneath her became a metal catwalk. It would be too difficult to cross it without alerting Anselem, so she watched him through its metal grating until he disappeared into a doorway. When he did not reappear, she secured her grasping hook to a joist and lowered herself to the floor. The winches in the forearm of the patrol suit made the merest whisper, the vibrations causing a small rain of rusty flakes to sprinkle down around her like an industrial snow.

Scavengers had done their work on the machines. Wires and wheels had been ripped away leaving behind trails of ruined shafts and stripped bolts. Sabrina stepped around the debris with care. Anselem had slipped into a large hole in the wall that looked as if it had been made by taking sledge hammers to the brick. Sabrina approached at an angle, remaining in the cover of a conveyer belt, her weapon raised.

Anselem's steps were receding. She slid through the hole and nearly lost her footing before she realized she had just entered a stairwell from the side. The scent of plaster and ceramic filled her nostrils. When her eyes adjusted, she realized she was in the entrance to the old subway. She remembered Sean was parked outside. A blade of light stabbed through the crack in the metal plates that had been welded over the entrance by the ministry. In the dim light she could plainly see the yellow-and-white tiles on the walls. Red ticket machines stood in silence, the only witnesses left of the people who had once poured through these tunnels. A sign, obscured with moisture and mildew depicted the subway stations running in a single line, southwest to northeast. Most of the writing was in blocky letters she could not read, but on one section of the sign not obscured by mold she saw letters she recognized but had no idea of the meaning of the words: *Haifa Carmelit.*

A chill overrode the tingling sensation from the suit's derm links. This was the old world, uncleansed, like an unopened tomb. Her instincts told her not to go forward. This place was forbidden. Unlike the shell of a house, there was no telling where these tunnels might lead. And yet Anselem was diving right into its depths. Someone had to follow. Her mouth was dry, and her chest seemed too small to contain the air she needed.

Sean would be able to see her heart rate. She took deep breaths to steady herself. An advertisement depicted a smiling man and woman, a child between them. Clouds of rot crept towards them from the edges.

Did they burn like all the others?

She remembered images they had watched in school of the Cataclysm. Bright white light, fading to a dark sinister red. A black cloud rising from a city transformed into a giant funeral pyre. Buildings turned to dust. Columns of white smoke rising to the stratosphere while people not obliterated in the first blast cowered and crawled, their eyes melted to ruin, their skin sliding off like layers of clothes.

Her visor vibrated, and Lindsey's profile picture appeared at the corner of her vision.

She cancelled the call, but in a few moments Lindsey called again. Sabrina cancelled it again, hoping Lindsey would get the point. Anselem was getting away. Her thighs burned as she moved silently down the stairs. He was walking carelessly now, even kicking a block of wood as he passed it. The turnstile's arms slammed as he pushed through. Sabrina took advantage of the noise and the echo to take a few generous strides forward before ducking behind a ticket machine. A rat scurried from beneath it. Anselem was relaxed, whistling even. She activated the grips on her boots and walked up the side of the wall, bypassing the turnstiles. When she reached the platform she was not sure which direction he had turned, the echo of his whistle seemed to come from all sides, but the flash from his palm light gave him away. He was headed up the tracks where the trains once ran into the highlands of the city.

A message flashed across her vision in red. "Sabrina, it's an emergency. Come to my apartment, quick—L."

What could have happened to Lindsey or her family? But as quickly as the alarm hit her, she partitioned it from her consciousness. She had a duty to fulfill, and if Lindsey was able to type a message and was home in her apartment, she was not injured or in danger.

Seats were set up in semi-circles for waiting passengers. Sabrina moved from one to another, using them as cover, until they ran out and she reached the end of the platform. The subway climbed into the hills above the city at an angle. Anselem was already far into the tunnel.

"I'm following him into one of the subway tunnels," she whispered into her microphone.

Sean's response was garbled. There was not good reception underground, but to Sabrina, it sounded like, "Affirmative."

She set her feet down on the rail and walked along it slowly. It allowed her to move more quietly than if she had walked between the tracks. The tracks were at an angle. She imagined the line running up into Hill 36, where she had caught Jacob the night before. Anselem was descending, his feet slapping the tunnel floor as he jogged downward. His footsteps and the occasional stone or piece of debris that he kicked made it sound as if he were right in front of her. When she clicked on the night vision of her visor, an emerald world appeared before her, the tracks clearly visible, as well as Jackson's lumbering shape, the tails of his jacket billowing as he moved. They continued for some time, through another station in which he remained on the tracks, but Sabrina climbed up and crossed using the platform before jumping back into the tunnel. Not long after that, Anselem stopped and turned his light back towards her. It was too weak to reach, but she ducked and turned the visor away, so as not to offer a reflective surface.

When she looked again, Anselem was bent over. His arm jerked and the tunnel reverberated with a loud bang followed by two others. Sabrina charged her blaster. Was this some sort of alarm? A wedge of light opened up over him, accompanied by the sound of scraping metal. Another man waited above. They exchanged a few short words before a rope ladder dangled down, and Anselem climbed up. The door slid shut again, and Sabrina was left in darkness.

Alone, she waited a long time, wondering if she had wandered into a lair or a trap. Red lettering flashed again before her eyes. Three more messages from Lindsey had come in a bunch, when she had entered the last station and had reception. Now she was cut off. She quickly adjusted the frequencies on her visor, shutting out any communiqués other than those from Sean but even the line to Sean was dead. He would have no idea where she was.

Unless she surfaced.

Her mind was made up. Sabrina followed in Anselem's footsteps, switching back and forth between night vision and infrared, until she found the hammer, the handle still glowing turquoise from the heat from his hand. Three crescent moons still burned indigo on the track where he had struck. Sabrina took a deep breath and pounded three times.

There were smudges of fading warmth on the door. She had not heard the passwords nor would the guard above know her. It was entry by force or no entry at all. As soon as the door cracked open, she fired the grasping claw from her forearm past the guard's head. Sensors in her glove told her it had anchored onto something, and she engaged it at full leverage. Her arm felt as if it would be torn from her socket as she flew toward the opening. There was a pain in her leg that felt like her knee exploding when she burst into the room.

The door guard fell back in shock. She glimpsed unshaven cheeks, a jowly face, and the flash of a knife before she fired her blaster.

He shuddered, the breath leaving his body in a loud gasp, his chest deflating beneath an old shirt with a checker design on it.

The grasping hook whined back to her and snapped into place. She was in a large room with rusting steal supports and high windows cloudy with dirt. A closed door with frosted glass led into the hall. Another factory shell. The man's spasms were subsiding. His pants were wet from the stun constricting and releasing his bladder muscles. She checked his pulse. It was steady, but by the way his eyes had rolled backward she was confident he was not waking soon.

He had been sitting in an easy chair, its skin patched by packaging tape. On the arm rested a tiny notebook with cramped writing. She took a closer look. She could not read it, but it looked familiar, the same writing that was on Jacob. Some of the writing was also similar to what she had seen on the advertisement at the subway entrance. She slipped it into her pocket as evidence.

She flexed her knee. The frame of the trap door had struck it as she had come up. When she took a tentative step, pain shot through her like a hot razor. She would have a bruise like none other. She limped towards the door and opened it slowly. Cool air blew on her face along with a strange, sweet smell that she could almost place. Voices echoed in the hall outside, but they were distant. A check of the infrared showed her no fresh footsteps aside from Anselem's and no warm bodies nearby.

She stepped into the hall. To the right was a blind, unlit corner. To her left, metal rafters hung over an empty space. The voices came from that direction. From what she had learned from the last factory shell, she guessed she was again in the office or control space that looked down on the factory floor. She moved in the direction of the voices. A control room was to her left. Within, a chair rested on its side and wires dangled from the bottoms of panels, their dead screens reflecting her silhouette. Her foot nudged a rusty screw that rolled across the floor with disturbing noise until it stopped against the wall. She held herself motionless, but the steady drone of the man's voice below did not waver. Paint chips fell in her face and on her shoulders as she pressed against the wall. She copied her approach from the last factory shell and dropped to hands and knees as she neared the corroded catwalk at the end of the hall.

One head appeared first, the head of the speaker. He was in a space cleared of machinery. In its place was a floor of polished concrete that was set aglow by rows upon rows of candles. Sabrina's mind flashed back to the evening at Joe and Magdalene's. That was the smell. But there were dozens of tapers down below flanking the speaker, resting on tall metal stands or cupped by glass sconces. He stood within a tight triangle made by three posts, each holding one of the gold, glowing symbols Sabrina had learned to dread: a moon, a sun, a sword. Surrounding the speaker in row after row were people. Sabrina was amazed that so many people could fill a space and still be so quiet. She was not surprised to see a semi-circle of a dozen in the front row, but the farther she moved onto the catwalk the more rows there were: bowed heads, upturned faces; teary, enraptured eyes. She leaned onto the catwalk as far as she dared before she gave up. There were too many, she could not see where they ended. The occultists filled the entire space, sitting on polished benches, throw pillows, or even beach towels.

Her palms left wet hand prints on the floor as she crab walked backwards. Sweat was dripping off her brow like tears. A green bar on her visor's readout indicated she had full reception. She stood up, her knee protesting, and hobbled back to the end of the hall. She would hide in the dark and call Sean, call for reinforcements, call the entire ministry down on this place.

She was waiting for her when Sabrina turned the corner. The rifle, an old projectile shooter, was pointed in Sabrina's face. Like someone as familiar with the weapon's workings as a solider, like someone *trained*, Lindsey chambered a round, the metal snapping and slapping with a crack that split the silence and echoed from one end of the factory to the other.

"Sabrina," Lindsey said. "I told you not to come."

THANK YOU FOR READING

If you enjoyed volume one, all volumes are available wherever books are sold online. Please leave a review, they help us writers a lot.

"When I have a little money, I buy books; and if I have any left,
I buy food and clothes."
–Erasmus

Please consider supporting the Equal Justice Initiative at www.EJI.com